OTHER BOOKS BY ZOLAR

Zolar's It's All in the Stars

Zolar's Encyclopedia of Ancient and Forbidden Knowledge

Zolar's Book of Dreams, Numbers, and Lucky Days

Zolar's Encyclopedia and Dictionary of Dreams

Zolar's Starmates

ZOLAR'S

Magick of Color

*Use the Power of Color
to Transform Your Luck,
Prosperity, or Romance*

A FIRESIDE BOOK

PUBLISHED BY

SIMON & SCHUSTER

NEW YORK LONDON

TORONTO SYDNEY

TOKYO SINGAPORE

FIRESIDE
Rockefeller Center
1230 Avenue of the Americas
New York, New York 10020

FIRESIDE and colophon are registered trademarks of
Simon & Schuster Inc.
Designed by Pei Loi Koay
Manufactured in the United States of America

10 9 8 7 6 5 4 3 2

Library of Congress Cataloging-in-Publication Data.
Zolar.
    [Magick of color]
    Zolar's magick of color / by Zolar.
       p.   cm.
    "A Fireside book."
    Includes bibliographical references and index.
    1. Color—Miscellanea. 2. Magic. I. Title. II. Title: Magick
of color.
  BF1623.C6Z65   1994
  133.4'3'028—dc20   93-23247
                                    CIP

ISBN: 0-671-76854-9

*This work is dedicated to
Dinshah P. Ghadiali (1873–1966),
whose lifelong research and
devotion to color was in our
time without equal.*

*And to Dr. Bruce Copen,
whose creativity in radionics
and energy medicine remains
unparalleled and is a constant
inspiration to his friends
and students worldwide.*

CONTENTS

A NOTE TO THE READER

The ideas, procedures, and suggestions contained in this book are not intended to replace the services of a trained health professional. All matters regarding your health require medical supervision. You should consult your physician before adopting the procedures in this book. Any applications of the treatments set forth in this book are at the reader's discretion.

ACKNOWLEDGMENTS

Hats off to the following for allowing us to include relevant material, without which this work could not have been completed:

The *Magic of the Aura* by Bruce Copen is quoted by permission of Academic Publications, PSI TECH, PO Box 291, Wadsworth, IL 60083.

You Are a Rainbow, The Color Work of Christopher Hills, edited by Norah Hills, 1979, is quoted by permission of University of the Trees Press, PO Box 644, Boulder Creek, CA 95006.

The Seven Keys to Colour Healing by Roland Hunt, 1971, is quoted by kind permission of the C. W. Daniel Co. Ltd., Saffron Walden, Essex, England.

Wisdom of the Mystic Masters by Joseph J. Weed, 1968. Reprinted by permission of the publisher, Parker Publishing/a division of Simon & Schuster, West Nyack, NY.

The Luscher Color Test, translated by Ian Scott. Copyright 1969 by Max Luscher, by permission of Random House, Inc.

Special thanks to Darius Dinshah, President of Dinshah Health Society, for his meaningful suggestions about the text and for permission to include a monograph by Dr. Kate W. Baldwin, and other significant material from *Let There Be Light,* copyright 1985.

And extra hugs to Nancy Engel, a good friend and great healer, for sharing her very special enthusiasm upon reading this manuscript!

INTRODUCTION:
A CHAT WITH ZOLAR

The tissue of Life to be
We weave with colors all our own.
And in the field of Destiny
We reap as we have shown.

JOHN GREENLEAF WHITTIER

Here we are again!
How very quickly the time passes.

It seems like only yesterday that I wrote my last book, *Mastermind Consciousness*.

Now we come to yet another level of understanding.

When the Great Master said there were "many mansions" (John 14:2), he was reminding us that there is never a single road to Truth!

To support this idea of the new universality of Truth teachings and their connection with esoteric Christianity, many students suggest that Jesus was actually referring to our current Aquarian Age in the following description:

> Behold, when ye are entered into the city, there shall a man meet you, bearing a pitcher of water; follow him into the house where he entereth in. (Luke 22:10)

In Mystical Bible Interpretation, the word *city* means our collection of thoughts, while the word *house* symbolizes our individual consciousness in which we "live."

In other words, we are instructed to take the teachings of the Aquarian Age—whose symbol, or glyph, is a man carrying a water pitcher—into our consciousness.

Not a single day passes when a new revelation, a new book, a new technique emerges, telling us how we may enter into that "house." Surely, there have never been so many "isms," so many self-help groups, so many seminars to teach us how to become that which we already "are" as right *now* in this so-called New Age!

For you see, in truth, as I have alluded to in my many writings, there can never really be a new age, since all that exists consists of the same, old Spirit! (Readers are encouraged to check out Thomas Troward's *Edinburgh Lectures on Mental Science*.)

Exactly what is happening to create these new ideas?

Simply this . . . just as a wheel shows no preference to which portion of its circumference touches the ground at a given moment in time, but rather simply allows each part to have "its turn," so too do each of the signs and astrological ages have their moment to touch ground.

Each astrological age is said to reign for about 2,000 years, bringing with it unique characteristics. Truly, it may be said that the monastery or ashram of the Piscean Age has been replaced by today's television set. Hence any organization that in essence is monastic, or secret, will find it hard going in this age whose glyph is the free pouring out of the waters of consciousness!

One need only to look to the Catholic Church's extensive advertising campaign for new priests, or the never-before public advertising of the Masonic Order, to verify this statement.

No longer must one "drop out" and go to an Indian ashram

to find Truth. Your local bookstore may have all the truth you may need, or at least may be able to handle! Hence Truth, like sunshine, is all around us.

It is simply a question of *carpe diem* . . . seizing the day (and the Truth) and making it ours.

So it is that I have chosen to approach the subject of Color magick from a somewhat Aquarian vantage point—by seeking that single thread that runs through all the rituals, namely the use of color!

Color is nature's way of telling us the exact nature of the energy (Spirit) behind every manifestation. Just as there are no accidents in the creative process, there are no chance events in the coloration of everything that exists, even the colors of our food and drink.

I promise you that in the pages to follow you will learn many wondrous things, especially as Walt Whitman once said, "You are not all included between your hat and your boots."

So find a comfortable chair and a good reading light, and sit back. Relax and begin the process of allowing color to speak to you.

Look around you and "see" for the first time what you have been looking at your entire life.

Why have you chosen to decorate with the colors you see around you? What is the color of the chair you are sitting on? Right now, what color clothing are you wearing? What colors were you wearing when you first selected this book?

For the first time begin to *see* and don't just *look*!

If you are like most of us, you have spent your entire life *not* seeing! To change your life, you must alter this conditioned behavior.

So begin right now, where you are, with what you have!

Your circumstances do not matter.

Just because you have only one suit of armor, doesn't mean that you can't polish it!

At first, you will find this difficult to do. (It was difficult for Zolar, too!)

But try . . . try . . . and try again and you truly will succeed!

I know you will be successful in this work. I invite you to write to me and share your experience.

ZOLAR
PO Box 399
Rocky Hill, NJ 08553

1

The Meaning of Magick

*Now Israel loved Joseph more than all his children,
because he was the son of his old age: and he made
him a coat of many colors.*

(GENESIS 37:3)

Perhaps no single word in the English language carries with it
the fear, trembling, and awe as does *magic*.

Webster's Third New International Dictionary assigns the following meaning:

> The use of means (as ceremonies, charms, spells) that are
> believed to have supernatural power to cause a supernatural
> being to produce or prevent a particular result (as rain, death,
> healing) considered not obtainable by natural means and
> that also include the arts of divination, incantation, sym-
> pathetic magic, and thaumaturgy.

An Encyclopedia of Religion by Vergilius Ferm further clarifies
this meaning by adding, "Use of materials, rites and spells believed

to be automatically effective for the fulfillment of desires . . . a practice based on the assumption that certain causes will produce certain effects not admitted by science."

The actual word *magic* is said to be a derivation of the Greek *magoi,* which was the name given to the Zoroastrian priests versed in astrology who followed the star of the Christ child. (See Matt. 2:1.)

The word *magician* appears some twelve times in the Bible. But while such definitions as these may explain *magic* from a cultural or linguistic origin, its real meaning can be found only deep within the psyche itself.

Carl G. Jung, in his book *Civilization in Transition* (p. 512), gives this unusual insight:

> But magic has above all a psychological effect whose importance should not be underestimated. The performance of a "magical" action gives the person concerned a feeling of security which is absolutely essential for carrying out a decision, because a decision is inevitably somewhat one-sided and is therefore rightly felt to be a risk. Even a dictator thinks it necessary not only to accompany his acts of State with threats but to stage them with all manner of solemnities. Brass bands, flags, banners, parades, and monster demonstrations are no different in principle from ecclesiastical processions, cannonades, and fireworks to scare off demons.

Aleister Crowley, perhaps the most famous of all British magicians, in his book *Magick in Theory and Practice* writes, "The question of magick is a question of discovering and employing hitherto unknown forces in Nature."

Eliphas Levi, yet another magician of note, clarifies this meaning still further by saying of it:

> A law exists which is ignored by the vulgar and made use of by the initiate. . . .
> Magic is the traditional science of the secrets of Nature which has been transmitted to us from the magi. By means of this science the adept becomes invested with a species of relative omnipotence and can operate superhumanly . . . that

is, after a manner which transcends the normal possibility
of men.

Levi's famous four rules for the adept, "To know, to dare, to
will, to keep silent," suggest that in the finality only the initiated
are privy to the real nature of magic and the workings of its many,
complex laws.

Traditionally, the practice of magic has further been divided
into two categories, which themselves are, not surprisingly, characterized by the colors white and black. White magic is that which
is utilized with good intentions by someone who is said to be "in
the light." Black magic is always used for evil ends. Although
sometimes it is difficult to perceive exactly which kind of magic
is at hand, the intention behind the act will always reveal the true
nature of its possessor.

Still another term for black magic is the "Left-hand Path." Here,
the name is derived from the fact that the extension of one's left
hand was from time immemorial considered a less than positive
greeting, as such might contain a concealed weapon. Hence, the
word *sinister* describes this other side of the human body.

Of this path, the occultist Dion Fortune writes in his book *Sane
Occultism* (pp. 117–8),

> Black occultists may be divided into two classes, those who
> deliberately say to Evil, Be thou my good; and those who
> stray onto the Left-hand Path more or less unintentionally,
> and having got there, stay there, often deluding them-
> selves. . . . The Initiate of the Right-hand Path is God-
> centered; the Initiate of the Left-hand Path is self-centered;
> that is the prime difference between them.

The magic of color may be said to correspond to that of the
white nature, and suggests an idealistic positioning not far from
Dion Fortune's definition of an adept as "a soldier-scholar dedicated to the service of God."

Lastly, there is little reason to confuse genuine magic as defined
here with the tricks and illusions performed by so-called stage
magicians. To avoid any confusion between these two "magics,"

I have altered the spelling of the former—magick—to agree with that of Aleister Crowley and others following in his footsteps.

Magick is created by spells. A spell is simply a written or spoken incantation, a formula, or the words capable of having magical effects. The word itself is of Anglo-Saxon derivation (*spel*), or Icelandic (*spjall*), or Gothic (*spill*), meaning a "saying," "story," or a "fable."

Spells, not unlike magick, are usually divided into various categories and uses, such as for protection, curses or taboos, injury or transformation, and the procurement of some minor end—for example, love spells.

The underlying belief behind spells is that there is a magical connection between the actual words spoken and the things signified by them. So powerful was this belief that the name of God was never written out by the ancient Hebrews. To speak it, or even write it, would be to evoke all that Jehovah symbolized.

Mention must also be made of charms, from the Latin *carmen,* meaning "song." These are simply magical formulas, sung or recited, to bring about changes on the material plane.

The practice of any magical rite or ritual, no matter how simple or complex, requires the belief that in some way there is a connection between what is being enacted and the Deity or deities who will carry out one's wishes.

For you see both ancient and modern magicians believe in God and magick! The latter, they often held, was in actuality taught to Man by God himself so that he could be worshipped, thus giving rise to the Law of Sympathy and the Law of Imitation.

The Law of Sympathy maintains that there is a mysterious spiritual link, or connection, between anything in the world and any one or more of its parts—for example, a tree and its leaves.

This is an important idea to grasp, since it will be seen to explain why it is that we can use color as the central, driving force behind all magick.

This Law of Sympathy has itself been divided into the Rule of Parts and the Rule of Contagion. The Rule of Parts says that even though something is no longer connected to something else, the fact that it was at one time so connected means that its connection can never be broken.

For instance, your nail clippings are no longer part of you, yet one can affect you by affecting them. This idea is the basis of the most primitive magic, or voodoo, which often requires that the hexed person be notified in some way that the magician has already begun to use his evil powers.

The Rule of Contagion is somewhat similar. This holds that an article once possessed, or worn by a person, takes on the qualities of that person and, hence, can also be used for magical ends.

While the rationale behind this rule is somewhat more difficult to comprehend, modern-day experiments in parapsychology suggest that some persons do possess a special kind of PSI ability that enables them to "mentally sense" impressions about other persons or events, from inanimate objects once in their possession or found at the scene of a particular event or crime.

For instance, a psychic gifted with this ability can tell you the characteristics of your deceased grandfather simply by holding his watch and "tuning in."

The Law of Imitation maintains that one can cause God, or the gods, to bring certain things about by performing a ritual in a certain way that will be noticed by the Divinity. A classic example of this is the ancient practice of pouring water over an unclothed virgin in order to produce rain.

If these ideas seem far afield from your own Judeo-Christian experiences, I suggest you take a good, hard look at the religion you are currently following. (Remember that the word *religion* means to "bind again.")

For instance, if you are Catholic, your faith holds and accepts the belief that a priest or saint can bless a medal in such a way that it will contain part of his or her essence, in order to protect you or fulfill your heart's desire.

Likewise, students of New Thought believe that through mental science treatment they can actually change their material life by becoming a co-creator with the Deity.

So, too, followers of various gurus or Indian masters may resort to varied breathing or meditation practices to bring about similar ends.

Eliphas Levi, in his classic work *History of Magic,* best clarifies our understanding of what magick really is:

> Magic combines in a single science that which is most certain in philosophy with that which is eternal and infallible in religion. It reconciles perfectly and incontestably those two terms so opposed on the first view . . . faith and reason, science and belief, authority and liberty.

In the end, it matters not so much what we do or what we say, but rather what we truly believe within our hearts—in other words, what we are conscious of. It is not so much what we have in our heads, but where our heads have us.

To bring these ideas to a close, we cannot find a better statement of Truth than from Dion Fortune in *Sane Occultism:*

> The difference between the occultaster and the occultist is that the former believes that the innermost shrine contains the god; and the latter knows that the God is within him. The former believes in revelation and the latter in realisation. The former believes in a special message to himself from his Master, a special mandate from Heaven; the latter knows that in God we live and move and have our being. The former believes in the astral plane as objective reality; the latter knows it to be objective imagination.

Now that we know what magick is, we can begin to look at its closest example—Color.

2

The Magick of Color

> *What a poor appearance the tales of poets make when stripped of the colours which music puts upon them, and recited in simple prose.*
>
> —PLATO, *THE REPUBLIC,* Book X, 601B

When first seeking the meaning of anything, language is often the best place to start. The word *color* or *colour* is derived from the Latin *celare,* meaning "to conceal."

Without going into the physics of vision and color at this time, let it suffice to say that, in all human experience, color is the most universal, and certainly most descriptive, of one's thoughts and emotions.

In the English language, expressions that reveal the occult, or hidden side, of color are legion. For example, who has not heard the expression, "She was green with envy!" Why green? Why not blue, or red, or purple? Surely, there is something in the truth of language that corresponds to the reality of the emotion of envy.

Later on when you learn about the human aura, you will discover that for some unknown reason the experience of envy causes the auric (electromagnetic) fields of the body to emit the color green.

But how did the ancients know this? Is it possible that those who gave us our language actually "saw" the aura—gifts which we as a race no longer possess?

"I was so angry I saw red" is another expression that is commonplace to most of us.

But why red and not another color? Here again, research in parapsychology offers a similar explanation, suggesting that when one is indeed angered, the energy of that feeling is "perceived" as the color red.

Likewise, when a person is "down in the dumps," he or she is said to be feeling "blue," or may even resort to "singing the blues" in an attempt to change the color of the emotion.

If one is a loyal friend, he or she is said to be "true blue." But on the other hand, if we are experiencing the feeling of love, we may describe ourselves as being "in the pink."

And, of course, there is no down as deep as being in a "black hole" or being a "black-hearted villain." Similarly, one can be caught "red-handed" in the midst of a crime of passion, or may exhibit cowardice and be labeled "yellow." Positive memories of the past are often described as "golden."

The unconscious association of colors with certain emotions was proved in an interesting experiment (reported by Orcella Rexford) children attending the Emerson School in Pasadena, California, were randomly given dresses and fabrics of various colors, and were asked to describe their feelings. The results were astounding, conveying that a "sense" of color is found worldwide.

Red	Angry, thirsty, mean, sore eyes, fire, danger
Yellow	Glad, light, summery, sleep, autumn, Easter, something didn't like (*sic*)
Green	Sleeping by a spring, cool
Light Green	Cool, spring, meadow, ocean

Darker Green	Cool, picnic, flowers, happy, swimming, summer, reading, lying down
Light Blue	Glad, happy, lazy, dull
Dark Blue	Homey feelings, on the water, happy
Brown	Woods, sleepy, desert, hog, mad, fell in pond
Purple	Feel fine, happy, glad, thirsty, happy world, sleepy, young, sneaky, run, queer, spring, in a flower garden
Black	Night, tear it up, sick, spooky, done something I shouldn't have, rain, dull, down in a coal mine, going under ether
Pink dress	Happy, gay, going somewhere, babies, apple blossoms, hungry, something happens that has been wished for, would hurry
Navy Blue dress	Snakes, winter, happy, love
Black dress	Funeral, lonely, sad, dying, walking in sleep, friendless
Blue dress	Mad, happy, glad, go for a walk, lonesome
Green-Yellow dress	Hungry, sick, riding
Light Brown dress	Autumn, fight, gathering nuts, woods
Peacock Blue dress	Gay, happy, water, swim, something cooking
Gray-Blue dress	Storm, rain, clouds, dull, pirate, happy

But this is only one example. Let's consider other documented experiments with color and behavior.

In an air-conditioned factory cafeteria that had light blue walls, the employees always complained of feeling cold, even though the temperature was a steady 72 degrees. Some employees actually wore their coats to meals, even when the temperature was raised to 75 degrees.

To solve this problem, a color consultant suggested painting the walls orange, after which the same employees complained that the 75-degree temperature was too high. The temperature was reduced to 72 degrees and everyone was happy!

Changing visuals from black and white to color can affect memory retention. A San Francisco college instructor, Richard J. Michael, found that when he substituted cool green slides for black and white, test scores rose as much as 40 percent. Two-color slides of red and green produced test scores twice as high as the black and white. Interestingly, using red and green on a blue background increased test scores by 30 percent over black and white.

What about color and suicide? Blackfriar's Bridge in London was world famous for its many suicides. The bridge was repainted green, and the suicide rate declined one-third! The Golden Gate Bridge in San Francisco (another suicide haven) is painted red, a color which traditionally inclines people to action. A coincidence? I think not!

Two groups of salesmen without watches were asked how long a meeting they recently attended had lasted (three hours). In a red room, the men guessed six hours. In a green room, the men thought they had spent less time than they actually had.

Alonzo Stagg, head coach of football at University of Chicago, employed two dressing rooms for his players. One he painted blue for rest periods and the other, red for pep talks!

The athletic director of the University of New Mexico painted his football team's dressing room in bright red and their opponent's in pale blue pastels! Hospitals have found that patients placed in blue rooms recover more quickly following major surgery.

Many years ago, commercial airlines abandoned the use of certain shades of yellow in their cabin decorations, after finding that these shades encouraged air sickness! Grades of schoolchildren have been proved to rise considerably when study halls are redecorated in yellow.

Workers in a certain London factory complained that the black metal boxes they were required to lift on a daily basis were straining their backs—until during a weekend they were ingeniously repainted pale green. The following Monday, many workers were overheard to comment on the ease of lifting "these new light-weight boxes!"

Dr. Gilbert Brighouse decided to record the muscular response of several hundred students under both green and red lights. Reactions under the red light were measured as "faster than usual," while the green light actually slowed down reactions.

A Chicago meat-packing house tripled its sales by painting the yellow walls of its display rooms green. Color engineers discovered that the yellow walls had been causing a gray after-image that made the meat lose its natural redness. The new green walls' after-image made the meat appear redder than ever!

Blue lighting in a factory that made women "look sick" was found to be the cause of excessive absenteeism. When the factory owners painted the walls warm beige, absenteeism dropped immediately.

Dr. Oscar Brunler, a Scandinavian physicist, found that mice placed in slate blue boxes became listless, while those placed in yellow boxes became alert and active. Brunler went on to conduct other experiments, including subjecting one group of partly intoxicated men to yellow-orange light and another group to red. Those exposed to the red light continued to drink, while those exposed to the yellow-orange lost any further desire for alcohol. Brunler hypothesized that the yellow-orange light had created a change in the chemistry of the liver since, when he radiated the livers of diabetics, they were able to lower their daily insulin from 145 to 25 units. Strangest of all was Brunler's cure of a four-year-old child's asthma, by his suggesting that her mother tie a red silk ribbon around her child's left wrist. Brunler had received notice of the near-death attack at his London office at 9:30 A.M. By 11:30 A.M., the mother phoned to say that the child was now breathing clearly. By 1:30 P.M., the child was sitting up and eating normally.

A physician in Pinehurst, North Carolina, Dr. Francis Owens, treated second- and third-degree burn patients by exposing their burns to green light for 30 minutes, after which the patients reported a dramatic lessening in pain. Owens also found that burns so treated healed far more quickly.

Insects also show definite reactions to color. Ants placed in a box illuminated by full-spectrum lighting will carry their larvae (normally kept in darkness) from the ultraviolet to the visible red. The color red, for some unknown reason, seems to interfere with the normal growth of cockroaches. (I wish I had known this when I was living in New York City!) When some 4,500 insects, mostly beetles, were tested by a team of researchers, the following statistics emerged:

1. 72 percent reacted positively to some wavelength.
2. 33 percent reacted to yellow-green color.
3. 14 percent reacted to violet-blue color.
4. 11 percent reacted to blue color.
5. 11 percent reacted to ultraviolet color.
6. Few were attracted to the so-called warm colors.

A yellow trap will catch more Japanese beetles than any other color. In Holland, horse stables are often painted blue to ward off flies. Shariff, an investigator in South Africa for five years, found that pink and yellow mosquito curtains did not harbor insects, while blue and gray seemed decidedly attractive to them.

Color preference among birds is unusually precise and appears associated with their feeding habits. For instance, hummingbirds favor red and will feed more quickly from red vials or containers.

With the exception of the human species, most mammals are color blind, thereby suggesting that whatever influence color has is not in any way dependent on its perception.

In the next chapter we will explore the mythology of color. In later chapters we explore in greath depth the healing properties of the various colors. It will suffice for the present to conclude with the following statement by Roland Hunt, in his *Seven Keys to Colour Healing*:

The fundamental laws and principles governing the cosmic energy we know as Colour have been ever present in Wisdom Teachings proclaimed by the Masters of All Ages, though beclouded in most men's minds until the days when the sun of our consciousness was strong enough to dispel the clouds of confusion.

Today, research and invention, philosophy and psychology, biology and biochemistry, physics and metaphysics are all uncovering facets of the jewel of Colour Wisdom, so long buried in its shining completeness, to emerge as the new Science of Colour.

3

The Mythology of Color

★
★ ★
★ ★
★ ★

O thou afflicted, tossed with tempest, and not comforted, behold, I will lay thy stones with fair colours, and lay thy foundations with sapphires.

(ISAIAH 54:11)

Everywhere we look we find the magick and mystery of color. In the Old Testament creation myth, the name of the first man is given as Adam, which means "red earth," no doubt suggesting both the color of the ground from which he is created and the red, firelike qualities of his essence.

Normally one does not think of earth as anything but brown, but such a color would have never sufficed to convey the dynamic power of the creative process in which these ancient authors believed. Early cave drawings found worldwide were painted with pigments often made from natural clays and burnt bones. Browns, blacks, and red are the dominant colors.

In the *Upanishads,* the early Hindus wrote:

There is in his body the veins called Hita, which are as small as a hair divided a thousandfold full of white, blue, yellow, green, and red.

For the most part, the ancients' first use of color was based on their race. The Egyptians chose red; the Eskimos of the North, white; the Orientals, yellow or gold; and the Negroes, black. To make themselves even more red, the Egyptians utilized henna dyes. With the passage of time, the use of color to describe a particular race or geographic area became symbolic rather than a reference to skin color.

According to the ancient Egyptians, there were but four races of humans: red, yellow, black, and white. Purple—not brown—was the color of the earth. The floors of the temples often were painted in greens and blues, symbolizing the ever-present Nile River from which all life was said to originate.

For the Tibetans, whose homeland was for the most part high mountains, their world view was similarly influenced. The north was said to be yellow, the south blue, the east white, and the west red.

Such color symbolism for the various compass points is found worldwide, regardless of the geographic distance separating various civilizations. In China, heroic guardians are assigned to each compass point. Mo-li Shou is the guardian of the North and is said to have a black face. Mo-li Hung guards the South and has a red face. Mo-li Ch'ing guards the East and has a green face. Mo-li Hai guards the West and has a white face. Should such ideas seem foreign to our Western minds, we need only remind ourselves that the Virgin Mary is commonly depicted in blue!

Tradition for the Navaho Indians maintains that the tribe once lived in a land surrounded by a special range of mountains that regulated both day and night. Again, those to the east were white, those to the west were yellow, those to the north were black, and those to the south were blue.

For many American Indian tribes, the colors red, yellow, and black were considered masculine while white, blue, and green were feminine. To the Cherokee nation, red symbolized success and triumph, while blue meant tribulation and defeat.

Similarly, the ancient mind conceived of everything in the world as consisting of four elements: earth, air, fire, and water. Earth was said to be blue; air, yellow; fire, red; and water, green. Likewise, all ancient civilizations assigned various colors to their principal gods and goddesses.

An ancient Egyptian text describes Osiris as, "O Osiris, paint thyself with this wholesome offering—two bags of green paint." The Roman Apuleius, in describing Isis, Egypt's true Virgin Mother, wrote, "Her garment was of many colors, and woven from the finest flax, and was at one time lucid with a white splendor, at another yellow from the flower of crocus, and at another flaming with a rosy redness." Horus was said to be a white god, while Set, who mutilated Osiris, was black. Shu, who divided earth from sky, was red while Amen, the god of reproduction, was blue.

To the Hindus, Brahma is often represented as red or golden hued; Vishnu is clad in yellow; and Siva, the destroyer, is black. Buddha, like Brahma, is depicted as yellow.

In China, the garments of Confucius are described in the *Heang Tang* as follows:

> The superior man did not use a deep purple, or a puce color, in the ornaments of his dress. Even in his underdress, he did not wear anything of a red or reddish color. . . . Over lamb's fur he wore a garment of black; over fawn's fur one of white; over fox's fur one of yellow.

In Japan, owing to the Shinto religion's polytheistic nature, has literally thousands of gods with their respective colors. The White Tiger, the Azure Dragon, the Vermilion Bird, and the Somber Warrior represent the four Good Spirits of Japan.

In the *Miyakko,* the following color-rich blessing is found:

> These white jewels are a prognostic of the great august white hairs to which your majesty will reach. The red jewels are

the august, healthy countenance; and the green jewels are the harmonious fitness which your Majesty will establish far and wide.

Strangely, the Koran has very few references to color, perhaps because of its somewhat late development in the sixth century, A.D. Green is associated with the World Mother, however, hence those who make the annual pilgrimage to Mecca wear green turbans as well as hold that color sacred.

Among the Druids of Britain and Gaul, there were three divisions of learning. The Ovate—or lowest—always wore green, which was said to be the Druidic color of instruction and learning. The second division—that of Bard—wore blue, symbolizing harmony and truth, and is often portrayed carrying a primitive Celtic harp. The third division always wore white robes, symbolizing the purity of the sun. This division ministered to the spiritual needs of the people.

These three (green, blue, and white) were exactly the same designations used by the ancient Greeks, suggesting that perhaps the legend of Atlantis is more than just a myth and that migrating Atlanteans might have been the ancestors of the Druids!

For the ancient Hebrews, the colors red, blue, purple, and white were all symbols of God. Sin, love, and sacrifice were connected with red, while glory was symbolized by blue. Splendor and dignity were symbolized by purple, while purity and joy were marked by white.

In addition to the actual scriptural mention of colors and colored gemstones, various colors have become linked traditionally with certain events. For instance, legend holds that the tablets upon which the Ten Commandments were engraved were created from sapphires, indicating their divinity. Likewise, a traditional red carbuncle was placed in the prow of Noah's Ark to guide him.

In the Kabalah, the Tree of Life (Sephiroth) can itself be symbolized as an expression of color. Kether, the divinity and Crown, is symbolized by white. The other two rays of this first triad—Understanding and Wisdom—are depicted as black and gray. The three Sephiroth forming the second triad are symbolized by blue (Mercy), red (Strength), and yellow (Beauty). The last triad consists of green (Victory), orange (Glory), and purple (Foundation). The final Sephiroth synthesizes all colors and ends in the color black (Kingdom).

In primitive Christianity, the Holy Trinity was associated with blue (Father), yellow (Son), and red (Holy Ghost). This idea is elaborated into the correspondence with the body (red), the mental characteristics (yellow), and the spiritual nature (blue). Still further, one can think of heaven as blue, the earth as yellow, and hell as red!

Tradition held that Christ wore a purple robe, symbolic of suffering and endurance, before his Crucifixion. The use of Amethyst rosaries continues this tradition.

Much of Christian art portrays the various saints in green robes, often with a gold or yellow nimbus surrounding their heads. With the onset of the Reformation, the use of color—like many other traditions in the early church (including ritualistic dancing)—was abandoned and replaced by the austerity of basic black.

Ceremonies also invoke the use of color as evidenced by that Old English rhyme that has been the dress code of brides throughout the centuries:

> Something old and something new,
> Something borrowed and something blue!

Last to be mentioned is the consistent use of color in heraldry and on flags. With the former, colors are called tinctures and usually consist of two metals and five hues, each having a distinctive meaning often gleaned from the various traditions of chivalry. For the most part, only pure colors are used with the two metals, with Or (gold) and Argent (silver) always taking precedence over the hues.

The hues are Gules (red), symbolic of purity and faith; Azure (blue), indicating sincerity and piety; Vert (green), suggesting youth and hope; Purpure (purple), royalty and rank; and Sable (black), penitence and grief. Somewhat rarely we find the use of two additional colors, Tenne (orange), strength and endurance; and Murrey (red-purple), indicating sacrifice.

There is also an association of specific colors with various holidays. For instance, the color red is usually associated with Valentine's Day and the Fourth of July. Red and green are associated with Christmas. Green, especially kelly green, is associated with St. Patrick's Day. Orange and black are associated with Halloween and Thanksgiving. Lastly, Easter brings yellow and purple to the fore.

Everywhere we look in the history and development of civilization we find both a consistent and often an unconscious use of color. Given this background, we can now examine the characteristics of individual colors so you may soon begin to use their magick to change your life.

4

The Characteristics of Individual Colors

★
★   ★
★   ★
★   ★

*All things manifest their potencies and their qualities
by means of color. There is a tremendous power in color
repulsions and color affinities. From these facts an exact
materia medica can be constructed. The seven different
colors in sunlight are each composed of a different style
and number of vibrations and each has special properties and chemical powers. Everything possesses a finer
positive and a coarser negative principle.*

—EDWIN D. BABBITT, THE PRINCIPLES OF LIGHT AND COLOR

While I have already alluded to the root meaning of the English
word *color,* it is important to note that in actuality there are
very few words in most languages to describe that which we so
glibly attempt to call color.

Hue (a synonym for color) has its origin in the Old English
hiw, meaning "form," "appearance," or "show." In Swedish, this
same idea is conveyed by the word *hy,* meaning "skin" or "com-
plexion." In Sanskrit, held by some to be the mother of all languages, we find the word *chawi,* meaning "hide," "skin," or
"color."

The word *red* is thought to be the oldest of color terms, its
Sanskrit root being *rudhira.* The Anglo-Saxon word was *read,*

which was most likely derived from the Latin *ruber* or *rufus*. While corresponding terms exist in every language, generally they were altered to suggest their attachment to a particular object, such as a gemstone or a god. In this sense, then, red and all other colors were considered adjectives, or descriptions of the tone (hue) of a particular object, rather than as a noun. The abstract idea of "color" did not exist to the ancient mind.

The word *yellow* comes from the Old English word *geolw*, the German *gelb* and *geld* (as in "gold"), and the Latin *helvus*, meaning "light bay." The Greek *chloros*, from which the word *chlorophyll* is said to be derived, is also a distant cousin. Here, the Sanskrit is *hari*, meaning a tawny or yellowish hue.

The word *blue* comes from the German word *blav*, and did not take its present English spelling until about 1700, at which time there was a strong French influence on the English Court. The French word *bleu* is itself thought to have been borrowed from German, the base of which is the Latin word *flavus*, which—strange as it may seem—means "yellow" and not blue at all!

Some scholars would argue that the origin of *blue* lies in the distortion of a Gothic word meaning "to beat"—that is, the color caused by a blow, which may be valid since we still have the expression "to be beaten black and blue."

The origin of the word *green* is simpler, since we have the Anglo-Saxon word *grene*. When one says the "grass grows green," however, all three words have come from the single Teutonic source *gro*, apparently from the Aryan root *ghra*, meaning "to grow."

The word *orange* comes from the Sanskrit word *naranga*, meaning "peach," which of course is itself a color. The Spanish *naranja* and the Latin *arangia* give us a clue that somehow the letter *n* was lost in evolution or replaced by an *o*.

The word *purple* is derived from the Greek *porphura*, an octopus which yielded purple pigments from which purple dyes were originally manufactured. Because of the rare nature of this color, once discovered by the ancients it became a symbol of royalty; one was said to be "born to the purple."

Not surprisingly, the word *violet* is derived from the flower of the same name via the French *violette* or *viola,* and is cognate with the Greek *ion,* from which the word *iodine* is derived.

Needless to say, the names for a great many colors have been derived from the source of their discovery. Examples of this include those derived from gemstones such as amber, coral, ruby, sapphire; from flowers such as rose, violet, lilac, daffodil; from foods such as plum, strawberry, peach, claret, burgundy; and from miscellaneous beings of nature such as peacock, canary, cardinal, salmon, fawn, and taupe.

Having concluded this somewhat rudimentary excursion into the world of etymology, we can now turn our attention to a detailed analysis of the esoteric and psychological meaning behind each of the colors, recalling that our ultimate goal is their magical use!

THE COLOR RED

Red is the favorite color of many people all over the world. It is the color of success, war, conquest, dominance. It is the color of blood, fire, the rose, and the poppy. It is also held as a universal danger symbol, hence its use on warning signs and stoplights, and has long been associated with the planet Mars.

In ancient Rome, red-haired puppies were frequently sacrificed in the belief that their passing would cause the corn crop to grow. In ancient Egypt, red-haired men were buried alive in the worship of the god Osiris. Fans of Sherlock Holmes will recall his "Red Headed League" adventure as well.

Being a universal symbol of power, it is not surprising to find the custom of "rolling out the red carpet" as recognition of visiting royalty. Similarly, Popes wear red vestments when celebrating the Mass, while the hats of Cardinals are scarlet.

Spiritually speaking, red symbolizes charity, love, and faith, and is often the color of martyrdom. Conversely, the color also symbolizes someone caught in the act of committing a crime—caught "red-handed," suggesting blood on the hands. Also not surprising was the use of "Reds" to describe Communists who were known revolutionary activists.

Interesting, too, is the use of scarlet bedding by physicians at one time to prevent the scarring associated with smallpox. Tradition at one time also held that the color red protected one against the evil eye. Red coral was especially recommended for this, especially in the sixteenth century.

According to the poet W. B. Yeats, red is the primary color of witchcraft: "the color of magic in every country and has been so since the earliest times." A persistent belief was that Irish witches wore little red caps, which they placed on their heads before flying to their covens.

Psychologically speaking, red seems both to attract and repel. For instance, some people fear others with red hair, following the tradition that Judas, the betrayer of Christ, had red or ginger-colored hair. Similarly, in India at one time members of the Brahman caste were prohibited from marrying a red-haired woman.

Red was often thought of as the color of lust—"though your sins be as scarlet, they shall be white as snow" (Isaiah 1:18); seventeenth-century New Englanders compelled adulteresses to wear a scarlet letter *A* as a mark of their shame.

Folklore holds that a "red sky in the morning is the shepherd's warning." A nautical tradition states, "Red sky at morning, sailor take warning; red sky at night, sailor's delight."

The Romans used a red flag in battle, while the Grecian god of war, Aries, was said to drive a red chariot. Mephistopheles (the Devil) was also said to be clothed in red.

Swiss psychologist Max Luscher writes of the color red:

> Red is the expression of vital force, of nervous and glandular activity, and so it has the meaning of desire and of all forms of appetite and craving. Red is the urge to achieve results, to win success; it is hungry to desire all those things which offer intensity of living and fullness of experience. Red is impulse, the will-to-win, and all forms of vitality and power from sexual potency to revolutionary transformation. It is the impulse towards active doing, towards sport, struggle,

competition, eroticism and enterprising productivity. Red is "impact of the will" or "force of will" as distinct from the green "elasticity of the will."

Contrast these remarks with those of Norah Hills, in *You Are a Rainbow:*

> The red level is purely physical. It is pure action, devoid of any thought. It jumps into the thick of it and then asks, "Hey, how did I get in this pickle?" A friend asks me, "Will you build me a shelf?" "You bet!" I reply. I'm off and running to the wood pile. I grab a board and my hammer and Bang! Bang! Bang! But it turns out that my friend wanted a glass shelf, not a wooden one.

When red is the dominant color, its possessor has great drive and forcefulness. Sometimes such a person will "see red" upon the slightest provocation. This is a person with tireless, inspired power. This native can create large enterprises from very small seeds. His or her qualities of leadership are superb, and this person's courage is without limit.

Should a Red move into the negative, shadow side of his or her energy, however, expect to see an emotionally passionate, explosive, and self-indulgent child, using anything whatsoever to gain personal desires.

Yet another way of looking at the various aspects of a Red is suggested by Dr. Bruce Copen, in his work *Magic of the Aura.* Copen suggests that one can think of the various colors as a musical scale along which there are three positive and three negative stages of development. Here are those for a Red:

1. Positive—Creative, ambitious, leader.
2. Positive—Believer in action, a builder.
3. Positive—Tenacious, fiery ideas to small endeavors.
4. Fluctuation—Vague fears, worries.
5. Negative—Irritable, hasty, fiery-tempered.
6. Negative—Lustful, intolerant, brutal and sadistic.
7. Negative—Cruel and destructive, black outlook on life.

Summing up the characteristics of a Red, Copen states, "The positive force of Red is creativeness and the negative aspect destructiveness in all its forms."

According to the Indian mystics, the horoscope of a Red is ruled by the Sun and the Manipura or base chakra. (Later on we will see how one can use the horoscope and gemstones to create powerful color magic.) Red is the color of the number 9. It rules the letters *K, L, R, C,* and *Q.* In the musical scale, it rules the tone G. In the four elements, it is Earth, and rules the years 37 to 52 of one's life. Aromatics vibrating to the color red are camphor, geranium, and sandalwood.

Dr. Max Luscher, whose works we have already alluded to, offers the following summary of the Red personality's qualities:

> Red as arousal, stimulation, as activity, fun, and creative willpower, is the symbolic color of a person who knows how to use his or her strength and ability. Red is the color of strength and self-confidence.

Finally, the poet Rimbaud suggested that a woman who wears red can be easily seduced.

THE COLOR BLUE

The color blue may be thought of as the antidote, or opposite, of the color red. Just as red heats, so does blue cool. It is for this reason that Edwin D. Babbitt called blue "one of the greatest antiseptics in the world" and went on to state that:

> When violent and maniacal patients were placed in rooms where the red ray dominated, they became worse and all their violent symptoms were aggravated. If these patients were removed to a room where the blue ray predominates, they became calm and quiet.

Blue has long been thought to be the color of the sky and hence was associated with the planet Jupiter by the ancients. I use the word *thought* since the occult Master L. W. de Laurence, in his classic *The Great Book of Magical Art, Hindu Magic and Indian Occultism,* makes the following comment on this point:

> Most people imagine the sky, in clear weather, to be blue. It is really white tinged with green, but the distance and clearness make it appear blue. . . .
>
> Professor Langley, says an Italian paper, has demonstrated the accuracy of his theory that the sun is really blue, its apparent color being the result of the absorption exerted by its vapoury atmosphere upon the rays of light as they pass through. That the sun is blue has been claimed by some occult writers.

Goethe, in his *Theory of Colours,* says of blue:

> This colour has a peculiar and almost indescribable effect on the eye. As a hue it is powerful, but it is on the negative side, and in its highest purity is, as it were, a stimulating negation. Its appearance, then, is a kind of contradiction between excitement and repose.
>
> As the upper sky and distant mountains apear blue, so a blue surface seems to retire from us.
>
> But as we readily follow an agreeable object that flies from us, so we love to contemplate blue, not because it advances to us, but because it draws us after it.

To the early Christians, blue was said to symbolize such things as faith, purity, and modesty, and the Virgin Mary. The phrase "blue blood" was coined by the Spanish aristocracy to suggest their superiority over the Moors they had conquered. Charles Perrault's *Contes du Temps* (1697) relates a European folk tale based on the crimes of the mass-murderer Gilles de Rais, who was executed at Nantes in 1440. So named for the color of his beard, Bluebeard was said to have murdered numerous wives and kept their bodies locked away.

A more positive side of blue, however, is suggested by Norah Hills:

> Devotion is the key for us blue people, whether it is devotion to keeping the skies and oceans blue and free from pollution,

or devotion to the growth of every living thing on this blue jewel of a planet, or devotion to God, the One source of all the colors of the rainbow, or even devotion to developing that conceptual part of ourselves into a creative tool for clear communicating.

Certainly, one can say that blue symbolizes truth, devotion, calmness, and sincerity. Dr. Max Luscher says this of blue:

> Dark blue, like all four of the basic colors, is a chromatic representation of a basic biological need—physiologically, tranquillity; psychologically, contentment, contentment being peace plus gratification. . . . Blue represents the bonds one draws around oneself, unification and the sense of belonging. "Blue is loyalty," as they say, but where one's allies are concerned one is especially vulnerable, so blue corresponds to depth of feeling. Blue, as a relaxed sensitivity, is a prerequisite for empathy, for esthetic experience and for meditative awareness. . . . It is the blissful fulfillment of the highest ideals of unity, of at-one-ness, a reunion with Gaea, the Earth Mother. It is truth and trust, love and dedication, surrender and devotion. Blue is the timelessness of eternity, representing tradition and lasting values, and so tends to perpetuate the past.

Blue personalities always carry with them a high degree of intelligence and often excel in the arts and sciences. Usually their mental development is along the lines of religion or philosophy. They are often quite passive and reserved in their nature. Poets, artists, musicians, writers—anyone who utilizes the imagination or intuition is often found among the Blues, which seems to be a coincidence of birth.

When the negative side of the color emerges, however, expect the warm, friendly Blue to become as cold as ice. Often, the world's snobs and social climbers come from this group, who now easily demonstrate their selfishness, hatefulness, and spitefulness.

Don't be surprised, too, to see this native frequently wearing various shades of blue as well as surrounding himself or herself with the same at home and in the workplace.

Dr. Bruce Copen suggests the various stages of the Blue personality as follows:

1. Positive—Artistic, knowledgeable.
2. Positive—A seeker, aspiring to mental attainment.
3. Positive—A teacher, loyal to self and others.
4. Fluctuation—Vague fears, overemotional.
5. Negative—Conceited, moody, emotionally unstable.
6. Negative—Cold in nature, snobbish, critical, unjust.
7. Negative—Cunning, weak mentally.

Summing up the characteristics of a Blue, Copen states, "The positive aspect of the color blue is intelligence; the negative aspect is ignorance."

Astrologically, blue is said to be the color of the planet Jupiter, and is therefore related to the Signs Sagittarius and Pisces. Its gemstone is the topaz. Blue is said to be the color of the number 6 and rules the letters *N, U, V,* and *W.* It also relates to the musical note A and rules the years 10 to 18 of one's life. In the four elements, it is related to Water. Aromatics vibrating to the color blue are syringa, lilac, and sweet pea.

Dr. Max Luscher offers some profound insight into the color blue:

> Blue is the ideal of unity and harmony. It is primal maternal attachment, loyalty and trust, love and devotion (hence the blue cloak of Mary, Mother of God). Blue is symbolic of timeless eternity and of harmony in historical time, that is, tradition.

To these ideas, Roland Hunt, adds:

> It has been said that Truth is all-conquering, and somewhat merciless, although this is more apparent than actual. Have you ever tried to live, say, for one day in an atmosphere of perfect truth? If you would realize the exact truth in all things, then you would be in perfect tune with the Blue Ray

and its calm serenity would be of great benefit. Blue is only fully used in a state of perfection.

THE COLOR GREEN

Green prevails as the color of beauty and harmony of Nature. For the early Christians, evergreen plants marked green as the color of hope and eternal life. And legend held that a man who drank the water of life turned green.

In the classic work, *The Golden Bough,* Sir J. G. Frazer relates various customs suggestive of the belief that the legendary Green Man of English Lore is a relic of ancient tree worship. In England, such a mythological figure was called "Jack in the Green" or "Jack in the Bush," and on May Day in 1894 was encased in a tall bottlelike framework covered with ivy leaves and crowned with paper roses. Later, English customs connected the mythical Green Man with Hollywood's favorite, Robin Hood, who dressed himself and his merry men in Lincoln green.

In parts of Russia and the Balkans, Jack in the Green became Green George. On St. George's Day (April 23), he led a procession, after covering himself with birch branches from head to foot, in which a recently felled tree was carried. As the procession continued, Green George was dunked in a stream or pond to ensure that enough rain would fall to keep the crops green in summer.

For some reason, too, green has traditionally been the color of envy. An old Scottish tradition held that if a girl was married before her older sister or sisters, she would give them green stockings, which might account for this universal idea. Along these same lines, an elder sister in the west of England was required to dance in green stockings at her younger sister's wedding. Stateside, an old American rhyme repeats, "To be married in green is to be ashamed to be seen."

Once again, our Master Goethe provides some insight into this color:

> If yellow and blue, which we consider as the most funda-
> mental and simple colours, are united as they first appear,
> in the first state of their action, the colour which we call
> green is the result.
>
> The eye experiences a distinctly grateful impression from
> this colour. If the two elementary colours are mixed in per-
> fect equality so that neither predominates, the eye and the
> mind repose on the result of this junction as upon simple
> colour. The beholder has neither the wish nor the power to
> imagine a state beyond it. Hence for rooms to live in con-
> stantly, the green colour is most generally elected.

Green shoots always indicate new growth and hope, continuity
of life, peace, abundance, and healing. It is said that doctors and
nurses often have green as a dominant color in their auras, about
which we will have more to say later on.

In essence, green indicates friendliness, cooperation, goodness,
mercy, faith, and peace. Orcella Rexford says of green that it "is
the symbol of energy, fertility, new life, growth, charity. It is
refreshing and cool, suggesting youth, peace and relaxation. The
expression 'green horn' indicates the youth and inexperience associated with green." It is only when green is darkened by black
that envy, jealousy, and superstition emerge, according to Rexford.

Roland Hunt adds his comments on this color in his usual
philosophical manner:

> Why do we send invalids "down to the country" to conva-
> lesce, despite better medical attention available in the cities?
> The fact is, we obtain actual material strength from the
> proximity of the expanse of greenery. It is an actual tonic
> to body, mind and spirit. It should be recalled that Yellow
> is the colour of Wisdom (Mind), Blue the colour of Truth
> (Spirit), and Green is the combination of Yellow and Blue
> offering a balanced body for both. It is because it is a tonic
> to the three main vehicles of the human-being that it is so
> successful a medicine.

Perhaps that is why the poet William Wordsworth mentioned
green twice as much as any other color in his verse.

According to Norah Hills, "Green is a level that we all experience at different times since we all go through feelings of insecurity and of heartfelt love, but it is the overriding, nurturing, Mother Earth quality that makes one predominantly a green level person. Another attribute can be the intensity of the energy, but that intensity, without self-mastery, can also drag one into the pits."

Dr. Max Luscher describes green in this way:

> Green corresponds symbolically to the majestic sequoia, deep-rooted, proud and unchanging, towering over lesser trees, to the austere and autocratic temperament, to the tension in the bow string. Its sensory perception is astringence, its emotional content is pride, and its organs are smooth (involuntary) muscles. Thus gastric ulcers and digestive upsets are often associated with worry over possible loss of standing or personal failure.

The Master occultist L. W. de Laurence suggests that green should be called "The King of Colors" since the Great Architect chose it for the universal color and Nature's primeval garment. Laurence suggests that "green has a soothing restful influence, preserving the eyesight and quieting the nervous system," and that persons who give it prominence in their dress are likely to be fond of travel and moving about greatly.

Most of the time, a Green person will be highly practical, down-to-earth, and quite natural. He or she knows the value of "cash" and likes to accumulate possessions. *Harmony, balance,* and *stability* are key words to describe this native. Superior self-confidence is often found in this color. Here is the bread basket for humanity. There is also a great deal of sensuality expressed in this color.

Unfortunately, a Green often considers his or her possessions of greater worth than friends. Once turned to the negative, a Green will become an exploiter and user of anyone and anything to get and keep what is wanted. Laziness and miserliness often accompany such a person.

Dr. Bruce Copen suggests the evolution of a Green as follows:

1. Positive—Harmonic, reformer.
2. Positive—Highly stable, a great producer of material things.
3. Positive—Practical, earthly ideas.
4. Fluctuation—Vague fears.
5. Negative—Tyranny, unscrupulous with money.
6. Negative—Miserly, materialist.
7. Negative—Greedy, no imagination, selfish.

According to Copen, "The positive aspect of the color Green is Balance; the negative aspect is Instability."

According to Edgar Cayce, green-yellow—or "gaslight green," as he calls it—is to be avoided. Preferable are those shades of green that tend toward blue, as these suggest trustworthiness!

Astrologically, green is related to the Signs Gemini and Virgo. Mercury is the planet associated with green and the emerald is its gemstone.

Green is the color of the number 8. It corresponds to the letters S and Z and the musical note D. In life, it rules that period from one's sixty-fourth birthday to the end of life. Its element is Earth. Aromatics vibrating to the color green are musk, benzoin, and narcissus.

In conclusion, the words of Roland Hunt serve us well:

> Green is the colour of Nature, the colour of balanced strength, the colour of progress in mind and body. Green stands for harmony, possessing a soothing influence upon the nervous system. Hence the deep meaning of those beautiful words in the 23rd Psalm: "He maketh me to lie down in green pastures . . . beside the still waters."

THE COLOR YELLOW

Yellow is often said to be the most ambivalent of all the colors. Related to the Sun and gold, it is associated with perfection, power, glory, and wealth. Yet in early times, saffron-yellow vestments were worn in church on Good Friday in memory of the

Romans' crucifixion of Christ. Early paintings often portray Judas, the betrayer of Jesus, as having reddish-yellow hair to suggest jealousy and hate.

In more ancient times, the color yellow was associated with jaundice and also its cure. Should a patient stare into the yellow eye of a stone curlew, it was believed his illness would be transferred to the bird. A similar belief is found in American folklore, which prescribed yellow flowers to take away disease. In Germany, gold rings were used for the same thing. In India, the ancient Atharvaveda contained a charm to take the disease from the patient and transfer it into a yellow wagtail.

Havelock Ellis, in his work *The Color Sense in Literature,* surveyed the use of color by various writers and held that only Edgar Allan Poe used yellow (and gold) in excess. Since such overuse suggests a disturbed mind, it is likewise not surprising to find its abuse by van Gogh.

According to Roland Hunt, "Yellow Rays are awakening, inspiring and vitally stimulating to the higher mentality—the reason faculties—upon which they have a very powerful and remarkable effect. Through enlightenment, Yellow thus aids self-control."

Goethe says of this color:

> In its highest purity it always carries with it the nature of brightness, and has a serene, gay softly exciting character.
>
> In this state, applied to dress, hangings, carpeting etc., it is agreeable. . . . We find from experience, again, that yellow excites a warm and agreeable impression. Hence in painting it belongs to the illumined and emphatic side. . . . This impression of warmth may be experienced in a very lively manner if we look at a landscape through a yellow glass, particularly on a grey winter's day. The eye is gladdened, the heart expanded and cheered, a glow seems at once to breathe towards us.

Norah Hills adds these comments concerning yellow:

> The difficulty in getting in touch with deeper heart feelings is very real for us yellow level people because our heads want

to rationalize everything. Heart feelings are so illogical. . . . We yellow types want to figure out how to change the world, but we don't always love the world.

Once again, L. W. de Laurence shares his understandings:

Those who lean to yellow tints in their dress or decorations are usually ambitious and intellectual, full of invention and original ideas. There will be an inclination towards speculation and a fondness for the grand and beautiful . . . with an inclination towards science and metaphysics or even spirituality. This accounts for the yellow robes of the Buddhist priests of India, for the ancients knew the true power of all colors. The pure yellow gives intuition, aspiration toward the spiritual.

Yellow to many of the ancients was the animating principle of life. To the Chinese, it symbolizes nobility. It suggests joy, gaiety, and merriment as well as the comfort and cheerfulness of the fireside.

According to Orcella Rexford, "A murky yellow is associated with sickness, with treason, deception and cowardice, from which the expression 'a yellow streak' and 'yellow journalism' come. For this reason, it is used as a symbol for quarantine."

Dr. Max Luscher says of this color:

Yellow corresponds symbolically to the welcoming warmth of sunlight, the aspirational halo round the Holy Grail, to the cheerful spirit and to happiness. Its sensory perception is piquancy, its emotional content is hopeful volatility, and its organs are the sympathetic and parasympathetic nervous systems. . . . Yellow's principal characteristics are its brightness, its reflectivity, its radiant quality and its nonsubstantial cheerfulness. Yellow expresses uninhibited expansiveness, a loosening or relaxation.

Yellow personalities are often found with their heads in the clouds. In a short time their thoughts will cover a huge expanse of various ideas. Very intuitive, this native is generally a very lovable person and is unusually generous. Whenever there is humanitarian work to do, you will find him or her busy at work. Generally good humored and broad-minded, his or her interests are often universal in scope.

Should the negative side of the color appear, however, expect a certain nervousness and self-consciousness. Here, one may tend to sulk and act unusually silly. Too, emotional instability emerges as this person sinks still deeper, producing sarcasm, forgetfulness, and shallowness. When this happens you will know it, for this unusually neat and tidy person will suddenly become a genuine slob.

Dr. Bruce Copen shares his understandings of the evolution of the Yellow personality:

1. Positive—Peaceful, high aspirations.
2. Positive—Tolerant and tolerable, seeks to do the good.
3. Positive—Broad-minded.
4. Fluctuation—Inferiority.
5. Negative—Fearful, brooding, resentful, treacherous.
6. Negative—Lazy, cowardly, careless.
7. Negative—Dirty habits, ignorant, perverted.

Copen says of this color, "The positive aspect of Yellow is expansion; the negative aspect is regression."

Astrologically speaking, yellow is related to the Sign Aries and its gemstone is said to be coral. Its planet is said to be Mars, and it rules the letters *I, J, Y,* and *G.* In the musical scale, E is its note. In life, it is said to rule the years 4 to 10, marking the beginning of the development of the mental characteristics. Aromatics vibrating to the color yellow are jasmine, cassia, iris, and citron.

Concluding our discussion of this color, we share the following insight of Roland Hunt:

> Those who incarnate on the Yellow Ray have a searching desire to acquire knowledge and wisdom. Their troubles usually lie in the gathering in of more than they can readily digest and put into circulation, both mentally and physically.

THE COLOR ORANGE

According to Orcella Rexford, "Orange has the vigor and stimulation of red combined with the gaiety and gladdening qualities of yellow. It symbolizes warmth and prosperity, plenty, harvest, autumn, glory, kindliness, expansion."

Both the pomegranate and the orange have long been considered fertility symbols, with the blossoms of the latter often used at weddings to ensure offspring from the union. An interesting love charm suggests that a man wishing to attract a woman should obtain a ripe orange, prick it all over with a needle, and then sleep with it under his armpit. Once this is done, he should give it to the woman concerned, making sure that she eats it.

Roland Hunt says of orange:

> Orange has a freeing action upon bodily and mental functions, relieving repressions; it combines physical energy and mental wisdom, inducing transmutation between the lower nature and the higher; it outweans moronic tendencies helping to unfold and raise the mentality—it is therefore termed the "Wisdom Ray."

Hunt goes on to say that orange aids in the assimilation of new ideas and that the color brings a sense of freedom from material limitations. For this reason, he warns that using too much orange can incline one to overindulgence. It must be used with discrimination, he suggests. As orange raises one's tolerance, it strengthens the will and increases one's ability to deal with the many trials and tribulations life brings.

Theo Gimbel says of the color orange, "It is a joyful color, protected from both the overstimulation of red and the detaching effect of yellow." Norah Hills says,

> Orange level love is a pervasive vibration of warmth and concern for the happiness of others. Maybe that is why the color Orange is so warm. You will find that we Orange level people express our love in an expansive way which serves our fellowman one way or another. The trap for the orange

level is pride, and our sharing may involve a "showing off" or "look what I've conquered" vibe. Instead of pure giving and radiating of our warmth, we may give in order to get confirmation from others. . . . Orange lives very much in the present like the red but has one eye on the future.

Generally agreed upon worldwide is that orange truly represents thoughtfulness and consideration. It is said that some yogis call this color the "soul of energy." Orange touched with gold is said to symbolize mental and spiritual ability, a high spiritual vibration that denotes self-control. Orange touched with brown connotes one who lacks ambition, one who is lazy. The psychic Edgar Cayce believed that those who have orange in their aura should be cautious of kidney disease.

The Orange native has tremendous energy that is displayed at work and at home. Usually he or she has been viewed as an "old soul" who has achieved a great deal at a young age. A love of animals and children is found here, accompanied with a high sense of law and order. Should the negative side of the color emerge, expect the native to become obsessed with athletics, especially blood sports such as boxing. Females dominated by the color orange are often the power behind the men in their life.

Since orange is a combination of red and yellow, we have here an unusual combination of passion (red) and mental acuity (yellow). Dr. Bruce Copen looks at the evolution of the Orange personality as follows:

1. Positive—Unlimited energy, believes in action.
2. Positive—Tolerant, warm-hearted.
3. Positive—Energizes others, love for all life.
4. Fluctuation—Inferiority feelings.
5. Negative—Irritable, self-indulgent, immoderate.
6. Negative—Sensual, sees no good in life.
7. Negative—Relies on others, lazy, always tired.

Copen summarizes his feelings about the Orange by saying, "The positive attitude to the color Orange is activity; the negative is IN-activity."

For some reason, Goethe has little to say about orange and does not even call it by name—rather, simply "yellow and red." "This is a somewhat preponderating combination, but it has a serene and magnificent effect," he wrote in his *Theory of Colours*.

L. W. de Laurence says of this color, "If in the aura of an individual Orange predominates, it indicates aspiration for the Self. . . . the Sun will be strong in the horoscope."

While red and orange both stimulate, orange has the property of both stimulating and releasing blocked or repressed ideas and mental traits. As will be seen later, it is an excellent way to correct these stubborn traits or conditions which fail to respond to routine psychotherapy.

Orange is said to be the color of the number 5, the letters *A, H, O,* and rules the note C in the musical scale. It is also said to govern the years 18 to 37 in one's life. Aromatics vibrating to the color orange are vanilla, almond, and clematis.

In summing up our discussion of this color, let's see what Roland Hunt says:

> The effect of Orange upon the mentality is to aid the assimilation of new ideas, to induce mental enlightenment with a sense of freedom from limitations.

THE COLOR INDIGO

Indigo is a combination of deep blue and violet about which few color researchers have suggested specific characteristics, save to claim that it is a color symbolic of high spirituality, having an affinity with the Third Eye, or pineal gland chakra, located in the center of the forehead.

Roland Hunt most poetically writes of this color:

> In the Arizona and Sahara deserts, the high midnight sky is often clear Indigo. Stars stand out twice as real, the air more refreshing than man's best wine. Drink deeply of this enchanting Indigo!
>
> Or, perhaps you have seen the scintillating Blauensee, the

Blue Lake of Switzerland, at the foot of giant falls. This crystal lake, and the trout in it, are of bright deep Indigo.

Imagine yourself, if you will, one of these free trout drinking ever deeper of the rippling Indigo water and light, flowing in and over your entire body.

Hunt goes on to say that this color is a great purifier of the bloodstream, as we will later discuss, and is a "tremendous mental freeing and purifying agent, controlling the psychic currents of our finer bodies." According to Hunt, "Indigo combines the deep Blue of Devotion and clear logical thought with the faintest trace of the stabilizing Red tone. So it is a Ray combining great power and practicality; one upon which sweeping reforms take place at all levels of our being."

Service to humanity on all fronts seems to be one of the major thrusts of the Indigo. Hence, it is not surprising to find a person dominated by this color in the church, the teaching profession, or civil service. While he or she may go unnoticed, a quiet dignity brings a sense of harmony to all that person comes into contact with. Devotion is always high on the scale of Indigo, combined with a great love of wisdom and justice. Rapid mood changes have also been noted when this color dominates. A female Indigo may appear gay and happy one minute and deeply sad and depressed the next.

If caught up in the negative side of indigo, the native can become a self-righteous snob, a pain in the neck to all around, and a rather decided hypochondriac. Religious fanaticism can cause such a person to dissipate all his or her energies trying to correct human mistakes in "God's world."

Of this color Norah Hills writes,

> The person on the Indigo level functions much of the time beyond the senses of sight, hearing, touch, smell, and taste and moves in that amorphous level of the "super-sense." Being in this visionary world, we indigo types sometimes hurt our friends without ever knowing it. We can become so spaced out and enraptured by our own inner world that

when someone is talking to us we don't hear a word they're saying.

For Theo Gimbel, key words to describe the Indigo are *overflowing soul* and *idealism*. Linda Clark suggests that the presence of indigo and violet as dominant auric colors indicates that a person is seeking a deep mystical or religious experience. Dr. Bruce Copen further suggests that indigo has specific psychological benefits:

> Indigo is a fine colour for removing Fear which has been and still is the greatest handicap. This colour helps one aspire to higher thoughts and tends towards a spiritual atmosphere. . . . In many cases where Indigo is required it will be noted that the mental symptoms such as Fear, Worry, Apprehension are most predominant, and unless psychological resistance has been overcome the colour lamps will have a long and tedious job.

Again, Copen suggests the evolution of the Indigo as follows:

1. Positive—A reformer, inspired speaker, or artist.
2. Positive—A seeker, aspiring to mental attainment.
3. Positive—A teacher, loyal to self and others.
4. Fluctuation
5. Negative—Prejudiced, self-righteous.
6. Negative—Liar, religious fanatic, self-centered.
7. Negative—Self-deceiving, disloyal.

In summation, he says of this color, "the positive aspect of this color is Wisdom; the Negative aspect being Folly."

L. W. de Laurence prefers to treat indigo and violet as similar rays. Of these he says, "the culminating point of electricity is in the violet indigo color. . . . Indigo belongs to Neptune." Aromatics vibrating to the color indigo are newmown hay, lavender, and balsam. Unfortunately, he assigns no numbers, letters, musical notes, or years in one's lives, possibly because the color is actually a variation of the blue ray, and is sometimes called indigo blue.

Hunt says of this color that it allows one to penetrate the kingdoms of the Spirit: "Indigo, the Ray of New Race consciousness, is his stablizer, his Light-bearer; it is the Ray promoting our deeper seeing and feeling into the true realities of Life, to make them clearer to our united understanding."

THE COLOR VIOLET

Here we come to the last of the original Seven Flames before the throne. While we later discuss the additional colors of scarlet, purple, magenta, turquoise, and lemon, it is important to note that these original seven hues (corresponding to the original seven planets) contain the essence of any other colors that might be created.

Orcella Rexford says of violet, "[it] is associated with sadness, piety and sentimentality. To the ancients it symbolized the raiment of God and sacred. It is a quiet cooling color." It is said that S. G. J. Ouseley believed the color violet is seldom seen in the auric fields, since it "indicates a very high spiritual nature, unselfish efforts and true greatness."

Roland Hunt writes of this color:

It is the ideal Purifier, and the Purifier of ideals. Its high rate of frequency is depressing to the moronic mind because its potencies are beyond their understanding; it is stimulative mainly to the Intuitive (Spiritual) nature. . . . Violet has great inspirational effect—e.g., the great works of Art, in Music, Prose, Poetry, Painting, Sculpture, etc. are indebted to the Violet Ray, the stimulator of highest human ideals.

Generally speaking, it can be said that Violet persons function at the highest levels of spirituality. Often they become inspired metaphysical leaders possessing high levels of mental and emotional balance. Original and sound ideas always come to the front when this color is dominant. Since violet is made up of red and blue, we have here the combination of creativity and intellect. When the positive energy of this color is in control, however, expect an effortless leader and gifted administrator. Such a person often displays a quiet dignity that is often sought after.

Should the violet ray devolve downward, this native can possess a violent temper combined with a high degree of cynicism. Treachery and unfaithfulness often accompany such a person, who is likely to become introverted, flaunting his or her powers over others.

Norah Hills says, "Violet is the world of the imagination and of unconnected, illogical images, magic and whim. It is the cosmic connection that pulls rabbits out of hats, paintings out of canvases, bodies out of clay, universes out of darkness, and creation out of the void; it snatches reality out of 'nowhere.' "

In Copen's evolution, the Violet person moves as follows:

1. Positive—Mystic, mentally creative, selfless.
2. Positive—Humanitarian, tolerant.
3. Positive—Leadership, loving to all men.
4. Fluctuation—Vague fears of power complex.
5. Negative—Selfish, spiteful.
6. Negative—Cunning, scheming after power.
7. Negative—Destructive, insanely spiteful.

Dr. Copen sums up the energy of Violet: "The Positive aspect of this colour is Intuition; the Negative aspect is Dogmatism."

Theo Gimbel writes of this color: "Here we meet two worlds, the relaxing in the Blue and the stimulating in the Red. It is, in a very special way, the colour of a consciousness balance: dignity and divinity, but also stability. It will raise the self-valuation and self-esteem of the person who has lost the sense of human beauty, and restore rhythm to the system." For Gimbel, the key word for violet is *religious devotion*.

L. W. de Laurence, as already mentioned, prefers to lump together the colors indigo and violet:

These colors seen in the aura of an individual may be taken to indicate various certain characteristics. Violet . . . love of truth, and all that is good, humility, zeal, spirituality.

Violet is said to be the color of Saturn, which planet will be strong in the horoscope. It is the color of the number 3, rules the letters *T* and *D,* and corresponds to the musical tone B. It is said to rule the years 52 to 64 of one's life. Aromatics vibrating to violet are carnation, menthol, and peppermint.

Roland Hunt suggests the following:

Leonardo da Vinci, the famous painter and one of the greatest investigators of the Science of Colour, maintained that our power of meditation can be increased tenfold if we meditate under the rays of the Violet light falling softly through the stained-glass windows of a quiet church. Wagner had violet draperies and materials about him when composing or bringing through, music of the highest spiritual quality. These instances illustrate the spiritual impetus which the high frequencies of Violet impart.

THE REMAINING COLORS

The earliest writings on the magick of color limit the hues to seven, corresponding to the color spectrum of the rainbow. Later investigators have added five additional hues or tones. So what we see in the development of color theory is an evolution of ideas not unlike that witnessed in astrology, which originally recognized seven planets holding rulership over the twelve Signs of the Zodiac.

Just as early astrological theory required that the planets Venus (Taurus and Libra), Mars (Aries and Scorpio), Mercury (Gemini and Virgo), Jupiter (Sagittarius and Pisces), and Saturn (Capricorn and Aquarius) each rule two Signs, so we find in color theory similar beliefs. With the advent of modern technology, however, various additional hues (like the newly discovered planets) have found their way into color theory.

For Col. Dinshah P. Ghadiali, one of the most prolific color experts, adding the colors lemon, scarlet, magenta, purple, and turquoise was a natural evolution of the system. While the physical and health characteristics of these tones are well known, as will later be seen, the psychological characteristics unfortunately are scanty. However, if we think of these additional colors as merely further combinations of those we already know about, we gain some insight into their probable symbolic meaning.

Lemon, being a combination of yellow and green, is said to be indicative of deceit, although as the color evolves into chartreuse, understanding and sympathy are said to emerge.

Turquoise, the combination of green and blue, is thought to indicate the compassion possessed by an evolved soul.

Purple, the combination of violet and yellow, symbolizes the union of body and soul, and reflects one who loves pomp and ceremony and who seeks ultimate grandeur!

Magenta, the combination of red and violet, is said to be the color of cheer and vitality.

Scarlet, composed of red and blue, is the color of pride, defiance, temper flashes, sharpness of tongue, and sensualness. Viewed in this light, it seems no accident that the central character in *Gone with the Wind* was named Scarlett O'Hara.

One color that has not yet been discussed, yet about which a great deal has been written, is the color pink. Pink, especially salmon pink, has long been held the color of universal love. Used magically, it can supply joy, comfort, and companionship.

The Rosicrucian Joseph J. Weed, in his work *Wisdom of the Mystic Masters,* is only one of many who have recognized this most important symbolic connection:

> There is an energy just as distinct and just as powerful as mental energy which for want of a better word we call "love." The warmth of the heart we feel for a loved one is the nearest sensation to the physical reaction we experience from this energy. Yet it is not sentimentality nor is it physical love, but something different and more refined. And it is a definite energy. To the astral senses it is quite tangible and pink in

color, not a paint or pigment pink but the pink of light, like a glorious sunset.

Weed presents a technique that combines visualization, feelings, and the will—a technique he claims will cause remarkable positive changes on the material plane. His steps in this process are:

1. Close your eyes and begin to create a feeling of love and warmth in the vicinity of your heart. "See" this as a glowing pink aura, which starts in the heart and then completely surrounds your body.
2. Visualize that person, group, etc., that you wish to help.
3. Imagine that a portion of your pink aura, in the form of a cloud, is going out to that other person. Feel the love for that person and see the pink cloud totally, and completely, encapsule the person.
4. Once done, immediately dismiss all thought of this process from your mind. In Weed's words, regard it as a "mission accomplished."

According to Joseph Weed, the daily practice of this simple technique, without visualizing or even wishing for a specific result, will bring about remarkable changes. One simply projects that universal love, symbolized by the color pink, with absolutely no strings attached. Not only does the person "receiving" this love find his or her life remarkably changing for the better, but the person "sending" the love also benefits. Says Weed: "Feel love. Send love. Encapsule a small portion of this Kingdom of Heaven, as Jesus called it, and bestow it upon another so that it may grow like the mustard seed in the parable and bring comfort and peace to many."

By now it should be readily apparent that while such things as "pure" colors exist, for the most part our experience of color is generally that of hues or tones. Thus, all color must be thought of as in a state of dynamic evolution from one tone into another.

While it will later be seen that most persons can essentially be symbolized by a single color, aberrations in that color reveal exactly where the person is in his or her material and spiritual evolution, as well as suggest probable health and disease patterns.

The list that follows, taken from radionic and auric analysis, was obtained by measuring and matching the electromagnetic fields of various persons and colors appearing in their auras, as witnessed by various psychics. Since research in this area is still in its infancy, this list should be used simply as a guide to suggested correlations between some shades of color and various mental states. Similarly, the continued desire to wear a particular color may suggest the dominance of a related psychological state.

The Red Group	Psychological States
Deep opaque red	Destructive impulses
Very dark red	Selfishness, low motives
Dark red	Temper, domineering, hatred
Muddy red	Unsavory cravings
Cloudy red	Cruelty, greed
Dull smokey red	Gross animal passions
Blood red	Envy, hatred, anger, revenge, jealousy, terror
Fresh blood red	Vigor, health, friendliness, love of physical activity
Clear red	Vitality
Bright clear red	Generosity, ambition, force
Fiery red	Irritability, passionate love
Light red	Self-centered, nervous
Red with black flashes	Anger, hatred, malice
Dull red with red brown	Fear
Red with much brown	Hopelessness
Dark red with dirty green	Greed, avarice
Ruby red	Vitality, cheer
Wine red	Sense gratification
Infrared	Black magic, negative psychism

Pure carmine	Human affection
Dull bluish red	Coarse passion
Crimson with black	Animal passions, low sensual nature
Crimson	Sensuality, passion
Clear crimson	Physical love
Yellow red	Rage, uncontrolled passion
Deep scarlet	Lust
Scarlet	Self-pride, defiance
Scarlet flashes	Righteous indignation
Scarlet-black flashes	Malicious hatred
Rose	Affection, love of home
Pure rose	Unselfish affection
Rose with lilac	Devoted affection
Rose tint	Unselfish love
Rose pink	Joy of spirit
Pink	Maternal love
Clear pink	Divine compassion
Shell pink	Creative love
Salmon pink	Universal pink
Coral pink	Immaturity

The Orange Group	**Psychological States**
Orange	Willpower, force, cheer
Clear orange	Companionship, extrovert, energetic
Bright orange	Intellectual pride, ambition, mastery through will
Yellow orange	Intellectual ambition
Dark orange	Overindulgence, lack of control
Golden orange	Self-control, intellectual development
Deep red orange	Ostentation
Orange with red	Power over others

Orange with brick red — Low type of cunning
Dull red orange — Selfishness
Orange with brown — Lack of ambition

The Yellow Group	**Psychological States**
Pure yellow	Spirituality, intellect, intuition
Bright yellow	Mental and physical stimulation
Light yellow	Higher thought
Pale yellow	Thoughtful, high-spirited
Lemon	High spiritual thinking
Sickly lemon	Average intellect
Mustard yellow	Low, cunning, craftiness
Dark dingy yellow	Jealousy, suspicion, selfishness
Dull yellow	Dreamy, visionary, impractical
Deep dull yellow	Tendency to selfishness
Yellow with ruddy	Timidity
Golden yellow	Happy, friendly, well-being, learns things easily
Clear golden yellow	High intellectual power
Rich gold with blue tint	Spiritualized intellectual attainment
Gold	Harmonizes feelings, soothes nerves

The Green Group	**Psychological States**
Bright clear green	Adaptability
Grass green	Color of popular music, money-making
Jade green	Tact, diplomacy, street smarts
Jade green with shell pink	Politeness, tolerance, polite deceit
Emerald green	Healing, eager youth, ingenuity

Autumn green	Desires possessions and distinction
Light autumn green	Intellect without intuition
Bottle green	Selfishness
Dark green	Envy, jealousy
Dark ivy green	Intense selfishness
Dull dark green	Total self-interest, envy
Dull brown green	Avarice, greed
Green with red brown	Selfishness
Green with red	Envious, desiring sympathy
Dirty green	Cunning trickster
Olive green	Treacherous
Light olive green	Popular writing
Apple green	Higher, active mind
Soft green	Peaceful, harmonious, home lover
Green toward lemon	Deceit, falsehoods
Light chartreuse green	Sympathy, understanding
Light clear green	Charity, sympathy
Pastel green	Individualization without selfishness
Pale delicate green	Sympathy, compassion
Green toward blue	Understanding others' needs
Pale luminous blue green	Evolved soul with deep compassion

The Blue Group	**Psychological States**
Bright blue	Self-reliance, confidence, loyalty, sincerity
Clear blue with lavender	Highest spirituality
Middle blue	Hard worker, achiever
Deep royal blue	Faith
Dark blue	Saintliness
Rich blue	Devotional feeling
Rich Delft blue	Serenity

Dull blue	Low religious emotion
Dull gray blue	Superstition
Blue with black	Fearful religious feeling
Blue with red brown	Selfish religious feeling
Blue with lavender	High idealism
Light blue	Devoted to noble ideals
Clear light blue	True spiritual unfoldment
Pale blue	Lacking depth but seeks maturity
Indigo	High degree of spirituality, seeker after spiritual truth

The Violet Group	Psychological States
Violet	Freedom lover, high intuition
Rich clear violet	High religious feeling, meditation aid
Purple	Body and spirit union, love of pomp and ceremony
Orchid	Illumined clairvoyant
Amethyst	Spiritual vitality
Lilac	Genuine altruism
Lavender	High spirituality

These are but a few of the correspondences found to exist for the colors, color hues, and psychological states. It is important to note that, with modern technology, it is now possible to compound subtle hues that were unknown to the ancients, who first ascribed the traditional correspondences presented here. This list should inspire you to "Think . . . Breathe . . . and Act Color."

In other words, you should become so familiar with the mystical side of each color that you automatically "think" of what that color means and stands for the moment you see it. It makes no difference whether the color is on an object or is being worn by a person. For instance, you already know that red is the color of action, so it should not surprise you that drivers or owners of red cars get more speeding tickets!

Start today to notice the colors around you, especially the colors you are wearing or that others wear. Believe me, it is no accident that a person chooses to dress in particular colors. But be careful when this person suddenly changes colors since this indicates a major change in personality or mental state. A similar change of mind can be gleaned when a person suddenly redecorates his or her house or apartment, dramatically changing the color scheme.

There are no accidents in the Universe!

Before we begin to magically use this knowledge of color, become familiar with the following Color Key. We are indebted to Dr. Bruce Copen for the idea behind this list, which allows us to move easily from a particular emotion to a particular color.

COLOR KEYS TO EMOTIONS

Key	Color
Adaptability	Green
Adoration	Rich dark blue
Affection	Crimson rose
Altruism	Bright green
Altruism (high)	Lilac
Ambition (achievement)	Deep orange
Ambition (intellectual)	Yellow orange
Ambition (material)	Bright clear red
Ambition (lack of)	Orange with brown
Anger	Reds of all shades
Animal instincts	Dull red with gray or brown
Animal passions	Dark ugly red, crimson
Attainment (spiritual)	Gold with tint of blue
Avarice	Dull red brown, dark red, dirty green
Awakened spirit	Pure white

Brutality	Red flashes on dark brown
Business capacity	Golden brown
Businessperson	Orange
Ceremony (love of)	Purple
Charity	Bright clear green, light green
Clairvoyant (illumined)	Orchid
Coarse passion	Dark dull muddy crimson
Compassion	Bright blue
Confidence	Bright blue
Courage (lack of)	Gray
Courageousness	Orange
Covetousness	Dark dull green
Craving (unclean)	Cloudy red
Criticism	Harsh yellow
Cruelty	Cloudy red
Cunning	Orange with brick red, mustard yellow
Deceit	Gray green, lemon green
Deceit (very low)	Dirty green
Deceit (polite)	Jade green with pink
Defiance	Scarlet
Depression	Gray green, slate gray, green gray
Desire (distinction)	Autumn green
Desire (possessions)	Autumn green
Desire (sympathy)	Green with red
Desires (low)	Crimson
Desires (sensual)	Dark ugly red
Desires (sex)	Crimson
Destructive impulses	Deep opaque red
Devotion	Mauve or blue
Devotional feeling	Rich blue
Devotional thought	Deep sky blue
Diplomacy	Jade green
Discord	Black

Discrimination	Clear golden yellow
Domineering	Dark red
Earthliness	Black, brown
Egotism	Scarlet
Energy (physical)	Bright clear red
Envy	Blood red, dark green, bright red with flashes of green
Evasion	Lemon green
Evil	Black
Extrovert	Orange
Faith	Deep royal blue
Falsehoods (telling)	Green with lemon streaks
Fear	Livid pale gray, dark red with black
Fear (hopeless)	Red with brown
Fearful	Dark leaden gray
Force (physical)	Bright clear red
Force (mental)	Orange yellow
Force (spiritual)	Violet
Freedom	Bright clear green
Friendliness	Golden yellow
Generous nature	Soft rose pink
Generosity	Bright clear red
Gloom	Black
Grabbing instinct	Greenish brown
Grandeur (love of)	Purple
Greed	Cloudy red, red brown
Happiness	Golden yellow
Harmonious	Soft green
Hatred	Black clouds, dark red, red flashes on black
Healing power	Bright emerald green
Health	Blood red, golden yellow

High-spirited	Pale yellow
Home (love of)	Soft green, rose
Idealism	Blue with violet tint
Idealism (sublime)	Purple
Ignorance	Black
Impractical	Dull yellow
Impurity	Dark muddy crimson
Independent nature	Bright green
Indignation (righteous)	Scarlet flashes
Industriousness	Golden brown
Ingenuity	Emerald green
Inspiration	Blue
Intellect	Yellow
Intellect without intuition	Bright autumn green
Intellectual ambition	Yellow orange
Intuition	Pure yellow
Irritation	Light scarlet
Irritation (uncontrolled)	Fiery red
Jealous anger	Blood red
Jealousy	Brown green, scarlet flashes on brown, dingy yellow, dark green, green brown
Jealousy (inhibited)	Muddy green
Joyousness	Rose pink
Judgment (unprejudiced)	Clear golden yellow
Logic	Pure yellow
Logical	Clear golden yellow
"Lone Wolf"	Heavy opaque gray
Love (human)	Pink to crimson
Love (impersonal)	Violet
Love (display)	Deep red orange
Love (nature)	Bright clear green
Love (power over others)	Orange with red
Love (spiritual)	Pure yellow

Low desires	Crimson
Low motives	Very dark red
Lust	Deep scarlet
Malice	Black clouds, red flashes
Malignant anger	Red flashes on black
Meanness	Heavy opaque gray
Melancholy	Dark leaden gray
Mental activity (high)	Apple green
Mentality (good)	Golden yellow
Mentality (higher)	Blue
Mentality (ordinary)	Dull dark yellow
Miserliness	Murky brown, brown orange
Murderous passion	Blood red
Narrow mindedness	Gray
Negative thoughts	Gray
Organizational ability	Golden brown
Overindulgence	Dark orange
Peaceful	Soft green
Perfection	White
Pessimism	Black, slate gray
Plodding persistence	Heavy opaque gray
Politeness	Jade green with shell pink
Power (spiritual)	Violet
Power (worldly)	Orange
Pride (ego)	Scarlet
Pride (intellectual)	Bright orange
Psychic powers (evil)	Infrared
Quick acting	Dark red
Rage	Ugly red on dirty green
Reasoning	Pale primrose yellow
Religious feeling	Blue, violet
Religious feeling (high)	Rich violet
Religious feeling (fear)	Blue with gray

Religious feeling (superstitious)	Blue with black
Renunciation of self	Pale azure
Revenge	Blood red, black clouds
Saintliness	Dark blue, azure blue with mother-of-pearl lights
Secretiveness	Black
Self-centeredness	Light red with gray
Self-control	Golden orange
Self-interest	Dull dark green
Self-reliance	Bright blue
Self-will	Scarlet
Selfish devotion	Dark brown on blue
Selfish love	Old rose on brown
Selfishness	Dull brown on gray with red brown
Sensual desire	Dark ugly red
Sensual thoughts	Red brown
Sensuality (impure)	Muddy crimson
Serenity	Rich Delft blue
Sex desire	Crimson
Sharp tongue	Scarlet
Sociability	Clear orange
Spiritual power	Violet
Spiritual unfoldment	Clear bright blue
Spirituality	Clear blue, lavender, often with luminous sparks
Subjective mind	Blue
Superstition	Gray with black, tinged blue
Suspicion	Dark dingy yellow
Sympathy	Pink, bright clear green, light chartreuse green
Tact	Jade green
Temper	Dark red scarlet flashes
Tenderness	Pink

Thought (higher)	Light yellow, primrose
Thought (sensual)	Red brown
Timidity	Yellow with red brown
Trickery	Dirty green
Understanding	Light chartreuse green, tinged blue
Universal brotherhood	Delicate rose with blue
Universal love	Salmon pink
Unselfish love	Pure pale rose
Versatility	Emerald green
Vigor	Bright clear red
Visionary	Dull yellow
Vitality	Clear red
Will	Orange, pure yellow
Wisdom	Pure yellow, dark blue
Worldly thoughts	Orange
Worldly wisdom	Jade green
Worship (with fear)	Pallid gray blue

Now that you are beginning to "think color," we can move on to exactly how this knowledge is put to practical use. We begin with something that is most familiar to us all—the magick and mystery of candle burning.

5

Candle Magick and Candle Burning

★ ★
★ ★
★ ★

"Yes," I answer you last night;
"No," this morning, sir, I say;
Colors seen by candle-light
Will not look the same by day.

—ELIZABETH BARRETT BROWNING, "THE LADY'S 'YES' "

Now that you have begun to see the connection between colors and feelings or ideas, you can begin to put this knowledge to practical use.

The magical symbolism of a lighted candle, being a single light source, stands as a constant reminder that there is truly only one mind, one law, one principle, one spirit in the Universe. This is not a New Thought, but a rather old one, for we find in the Bible (Exodus 25 and 37) that God instructed Moses to make a seven-branched golden candlestick, or Menorah. Later on, an angel tells Zechariah that "these seven are the eyes of the Lord, which range through the whole earth." Some scholars would have us believe that the "seven eyes" are the seven planets, or that the seven branches of the candlestick symbolize God's creation of the world. In any event, the connection between God and the light from burning candles is indeed an ancient one.

In the fourth century, the Christian writer Lactantius severely criticized the practice of worshipping God by lighting candles because it implied that God was in darkness. He went on to suggest that if instead the worshipper contemplated the sun in the heavens, he would soon realize that God had no need of candles. Obviously, most present-day Christians are unaware of these wry comments, since the use of candles in churches is almost universal. In fact, the Christian festival of Candlemas (February 2) commemorates the Purification of the Virgin Mary, when she took the baby Jesus to the Temple and was told that he would grow up to be "a light to lighten the Gentiles."

Symbolically speaking, light and darkness represent a pair of opposites that have always had great meaning to students on the Path. Modern magicians are in agreement that kindling any fire—or lighting candles of any kind—should never be done indifferently or with a lack of reverence.

Whenever candles are used for magical ends, the room should first be placed in total darkness. Later, when this darkness is banished by lighting a candle, the act symbolizes the power entrusted to humankind—a power said to "Make Suns on earth." In truth, the power in our ability to create light lies deep within the unconscious mind, which may recall as a race memory that first moment when human beings discovered fire—symbolic of joy, newness, and warmth.

While people with Judeo-Christian roots would like to think of candles (and fire) as exclusively their own, the real origin of such practices lies hidden in ancient mysteries, which far too often are unfortunately called pagan or heathen. Interesting proof of this is that one of the traditional names given to the Devil is Lucifer, which means simply "light-bearer."

When we say that candle burning is a magical practice, we mean only that its regular, systematic use can bring about changes in one's life that are not so easily explained by reason or logic. But these changes can be created only with a planned, definite desire to bring them about. For instance, anyone who burns candles must know *exactly* what it is he or she desires. Burning a candle is an act of energizing the will and desire through spiritual means. As the candle burns under the watchful eye of the worshipper, its light begins the alchemical transference of matter into Spirit, only to return to matter once again as the desire is manifested.

The rule for candle burning is simple: Burn a candle of a specific color for the same purpose seven days in a row at the same time of day in the same room. Once the seven days have passed, rest for three days and if necessary begin again. It is also important that the commencement of any candle-burning ritual start on the day for which the planetary rulership corresponds with the desired end of the ritual.

Following is a list of the days of the week, the planets ruling them, and their general characteristics.

Day of the Week	Planet Ruling	Characteristics
Sunday	Sun (red or gold)	Men— Fame, health, job advancement, success, any person in authority
Monday	Moon (orange or silver)	Women— Emotional things, home, employees

Tuesday	Mars (yellow)	Sex, energy, passion, enemies, self-confidence
Wednesday	Mercury (green)	Letters, telephone calls, mental ability, academic studies, communication
Thursday	Jupiter (blue)	Legal matters, business, finances, protection, spirituality, honor, physicians
Friday	Venus (indigo)	Love affairs, beauty, female friends, marriage, art and music, children
Saturday	Saturn (violet, black)	Obstructions, delays, destruction, real estate

Remember—burning candles is a serious business and should always be conducted with reverence.

Find a quiet, private place in which to set up an altar of sorts, upon which will be placed:

- A candle holder or holders
- Matches to light the candles
- An incense burner and incense (if desired)
- A small dish of vegetable oil
- A knife, needle, or ballpoint pen
- Candles required.

Remember that every time you perform this ritual you must use a new candle. For this reason you may wish to purchase a dozen or so candles to have on hand before you begin.

In addition, you may wish to obtain a scarf, preferably white, upon which you will place various implements. And you may wish to obtain a small mirror, which will be placed behind the candles, in which you can see your reflection. While the mirror is not absolutely necessary, it has been found to increase the success of the rituals.

It is absolutely imperative to the success of any candle burning that the candle of the correct color be burned and that the burning commence on the correct planetary day. For example, let us suppose that you wish to influence the outcome of a lawsuit. Lawsuits are ruled by Jupiter, whose day is Thursday and whose candle color is blue. This means that you will start your candle burning on Thursday and will use a blue candle.

Once you have selected the day and the color candle required, it is important that you select a specific time to commence your burning ritual. While it does not matter what time of day you select—as long as you can darken the room in which the ritual takes place—the time must be when you can perform your ceremony each of the seven days. In other words, it is not advisable to begin your ritual at 7 P.M. on one day and then switch to another time the next day.

Whatever time you decide upon initially, you must adhere throughout. The reason for this is simple. When you perform your candle-burning ceremony, you impress your wishes and desires upon the Universal Mind, of which you are a part. This is done most easily if you create a specific mental habit that combines both concentration and anticipation of the outcome you wish to achieve. When you perform your ritual in the same place at the same time, your unconscious mind is already programed to accept those thoughts which you place in it. This is what's behind the magick. Your candle-burning ritual simply enables you to contact that part of yourself, which then does the work.

Whether you use incense or not is also a personal choice. Many persons feel more relaxed, more reverent, when incense is burned. On the other hand, should the smell of incense bother you, simply discontinue its use. In no way will the incense affect the success of your ceremony.

As with choosing a definite time, you must also find a definite space that can always be used for candle burning. This need not be an entire room, but it must be a space that can be darkened and where you will not be disturbed. It can be a space used for other things as well—for instance, a small lamp table or a dresser. The important thing is that it can be used each and every time!

When it comes to the candles themselves, you must use the correct color candle if you wish to be successful. Never substitute one color candle for another. Every time you perform your candle-burning ceremony, you should use a new candle, even if you have one that has been only partly used. In this way you pay respect to the candle, its color, and the planetary lord who rules over it.

There is only one exception to this rule: A white candle can be used in place of another, if absolutely necessary. When this is done, however, mark the proper color's name on the substitute candle with a needle, ballpoint pen, or tip of a sharp knife. For example, should you use a white candle in place of a blue one, engrave the word *blue* on the side of the candle near the end that is placed in the holder.

As for the candle holder or holders, they can be made of metal, glass, or wood. If glass or ceramic, however, they should be crystal (clear glass) or white ceramic. They can be of any height, shape, or design.

Once you have purchased your candles and brought them home, you must clean and bless them before they are used. To do this, simply hold each candle in turn by its base (the part that goes into the holder) under running tap water while you say the following:

> *Light of Lights and Light of My Life,*
> *I Cleanse and Bless You to Do My Service*
> *Which Is Thy Service. And so it is!*

After repeating this blessing, set each candle aside to dry so it will be ready to use when needed.

Now you are ready to begin your candle-burning ceremony. A reminder before you begin, you have:

1. Selected the correct color candle to match the work you are doing.
2. Selected the correct day of the week upon which to begin this work.
3. Selected a time to begin your ritual that you can maintain every day for the next seven days.
4. Selected a place that can be darkened where you can do your ceremony undisturbed.
5. Selected all the implements—matches, incense, etc.— needed for your work. You have even put the cat out and turned the telephone off.

Now you are ready to begin!

Take your candle and with a ballpoint pen, needle, or tip of a knife, scratch on the candle the name of the person or a word to describe the wish you would like fulfilled. If a person, use his or her first name or initials. If you do not know the person's name, but only the person's sex, simply ascribe the word *him* or *her*.

If you are seeking fulfillment of some wish or desire, simplify it to a single word—for example, "More money" or just "Money" or "Luck" or "A new lover." By making this inscription on the candle, you are magically transforming it into the person you wish to contact or the thing you wish to obtain. This is the first step toward gaining power over that which you wish to have happen in your life!

Now you must dress your candle.

Dab a small amount of vegetable oil on your fingers and apply it to the candle's center, then move upward toward the wick. Then go back to the center and move downward toward the candle's base. Do *not* go from the top of the candle to the bottom in one pass, or from the bottom to the top. You must start at the center and move as directed.

As you anoint your candle, think of that thing you wish to obtain from this ceremony. In the next chapter we will share with you rituals that cover most of the situations you may wish to effect with this work. Before going on to that chapter, however, carefully read again the instructions presented thus far, since your success in this work will depend on your understanding of these basic steps.

6

Candle-Burning Rituals

★
★
★
★
★
★
★

For memory has painted this perfect day
With colors that never fade
And we find at the end of a perfect day
The soul of a friend we've made.

—CARRIE JACOBS BOND, "A PERFECT DAY"

The rituals that follow, while very simple, are unusually powerful in their ability to execute changes in one's life. Remember, however, that they work because you work them, and that all color is God's gift, which when we understand, we can use!

To make your work as simple as possible, I have first divided these rituals into broad categories such as love, health, and prosperity. Within each of these major categories are various subcategories that will cover many situations you will encounter once you begin this work. In some of the rituals you will find an optional suggestion that you read a particular Bible psalm in conjunction with the candle burning. As with using incense, this is an option you may or may not wish to do.

One final comment. To get the best results from each candle

burning, set aside an hour's time for each ceremony. After the hour, simply extinguish the candle (or candles), put away your tools, and go about your daily business.

LOVE

To Attract Love

Candle color	If you are a woman, use a yellow candle. If you are a man, use an indigo candle.
Day of the week	If you are a woman, begin on Tuesday. If you are a man, begin on Friday.
Affirmation	"It's me you love, I know it's true. It's me you love, You know it too!"
	Repeat this aloud *seven* times while the candle continues to burn. Be sure that you have engraved *his* or *her* initials on the candle!
Optional	Read Psalm 138, "I will praise Thee."

To Save a Marriage or Partnership

Candle color	Green
Day of the week	Friday
Affirmation	"A love like ours was meant to be, It's me for you and you for me. And no others do we see. Together, Together, Together WE . . . WE . . . WE."
	Repeat this aloud *seven* times while the candle continues to burn.
Optional	Read Psalm 139, "O Lord Thou has searched me."

To Repair a Broken Love Affair

Candle color	Indigo
Day of the week	Friday
Affirmation	Our love is not a sometimes thing, Our love is like a diamond ring. No anger do I hold toward you, No doubt do I possess. So you now come back and always know That it's YOU I love the best!"
	Repeat aloud *seven* times while the candle continues to burn.
Optional	Read Psalm 85 while facing south, "Lord, Thou has been favorable."

To Make More Friends

Candle color	Red or gold
Day of the week	Sunday
Affirmation	"New friends I make, new friends I keep. For me they feel my love. In them I see the Christ in Me, And know my Father's above."
	Repeat this aloud *nine* times while the candle continues to burn.
Optional	Read Psalm 133, "Behold how good and how pleasant."

For Peace in the Home

Candle color   Blue

Day of the week   Thursday

Affirmation   "Happiness now burns in this house,
And Peace and Love abound.
For all who enter here,
Green pastures are always found.
This is OUR HOME, our PLACE OF
   PEACE.
Our Place of QUIET and CALM.
All hurts have been healed once
   We enter here.
Our fear is long since gone."

Repeat this aloud *three* times while the candle continues to burn.

To Arouse Sexual Passion

Candle color   Red

Day of the week   Tuesday

Affirmation   "I'm hot for you,
You're hot for me
This is the Truth,
We both see.
So COME . . . COME,
This you can't DENY
Don't bother to ask the reason 'Why!'

Repeat this aloud *nine* times while the candle continues to burn.

There is no Psalm recommended.

To Break Up a Love Affair

Candle color   Violet or black

Day of the week   Saturday

Affirmation   "Here is one half of the pair,
     Now his (her) love nest
       Will soon be bare.
     Who's half of the whole
       Will soon be single
     And the Gold in my heart
       Will jangle jingle.
     For what seemed attractive
       Now seems plain
     And what was Sunshine
       Has now turned to rain."

Repeat this aloud *nine* times while the candle continues to burn. Be sure that you inscribe the name or the initials of the person whom you wish to "do the leaving" on the candle. If you yourself are trying to leave, but haven't been able to, place your own initials on this candle.

Optional   Read Psalm 3, "Lord, how are they."

PROSPERITY

To Get a New Job

Candle color   Red or gold

Day of the week   Sunday

Affirmation   "I have a wonderful new job,
     For wonderful pay

It comes to me now
　In a wonderful way.
It's the right job for right NOW,
　It's the right job for me.
I simply open my eyes
　For my Faith is in Thee."

Repeat this aloud *eight* times while the candle continues to burn.

Optional　　　　　Read Psalm 8, "O Lord our Lord."

For a Job Promotion

Candle color　　　Red or gold

Day of the week　Sunday

Affirmation　　　"Like a giant balloon,
　To the heavens I soar.
　Climbing three steps at a time,
　I now make the touchdown score
　To claim the job that is mine
　That is waiting for me . . .
　What others envy, I now
　　'See.' "

Repeat aloud *eight* times while the candle continues to burn.

Optional　　　　　Read Psalm 92, "It is a good thing."

To Find Fulfillment at Work

Candle color	Green
Day of the week	Friday
Affirmation	"Green is the color that makes things grow, Green is the color of business and 'dough.' I give wonderful service in a wonderful way So when it comes time to harvest, There's plenty of hay."
	Repeat aloud *eight* times while the candle continues to burn.
Optional	Read Psalm 122, "I was glad when."

To Win a Lawsuit

Candle color	Blue
Day of the week	Thursday
Affirmation	"To grant the judgment that I seek, I turn within this day. And ask that fairness and equity Be the tunes that now play. Knowing well that what I ask for Is what should really be, I rest in peace and turn my trust TO THEE and THEE and THEE!"
	Repeat aloud *three* times while the candle continues to burn.
Optional	Read Psalm 5, "Give ear to my words."

To Win a Contest or Lottery

Candle color   Green

Day of the week   Friday

Affirmation   "O Lady Luck come to me Now,
                    And bring me what I need.
                    I've got the Sun, I want the rain,
                    I've planted all my seed.
                    So bring me a WIN and let me cash in,
                    The Tickets I now hold.
                    For I promise you I'll do my share
                    To help others still out in the cold!"

                    Repeat aloud *eight* times while the candle
                    continues to burn.

Optional   Read Psalm 4, "Hear me when I call."

To Sell a House

Candle color   Green

Day of the week   Friday

Affirmation   "A house is not a home
                    If it's time for me to roam.
                    So I let go right now,
                    Knowing that milk is not the cow.
                    A new place waits for me,
                    And for my loved ones too.
                    So I let you take this house,
                    To do with what YOU WILL!"

Optional   Read Psalm 61, "Hear my cry, O God."

To Win Over a Landlord

Candle color   Violet or black

Day of the week	Saturday

Affirmation

"Your words, Your Acts, Your Promises,
   Have never sounded true.
And so it's time that you get Yours,
   Right in the Kazoo!
For one who lives for profit alone,
   Will never find his place.
So here's a piece of that pie you stole,
   Right in the face!"

Repeat aloud *nine* times while the candle continues to burn.

Optional   Read Psalm 74, "O God why hast you."

To Become Pregnant

Candle color	Green
Day of the week	Friday

Affirmation

"Lord of Darkness, Lord of Light,
Let me conceive this very night.
Bring me a strong and healthy child,
Make him (her) rich, wise, and wild.
Give him (her) Fame and Truth and Smiles.
That he (she) might serve THEE all the
   while."

Repeat this aloud *seven* times while the candle continues to burn.

Optional   Read Psalm 103, "Bless the Lord, O my soul."

To Find a New Home

Candle color	Orange or silver

Day of the week   Monday

Affirmation

"For everything there is a place,
For everyone there is a space.
For me and mine, there is a home
In which to rest, to pray and roam.
For this I THANK YOU knowing well
That my new home now rings its bell!"

Repeat this aloud *three* times while the candle continues to burn.

Optional   Read Psalm 61, "Hear my cry, O God."

PROTECTION

For a Loved One Who Is Away

Candle color   Orange or silver

Day of the week   Monday

Affirmation

"Although you're out of sight,
You're never out of mind.
The God that guides your journey,
Is always one who's kind.
It's HE who goes before you
To make the crooked straight.
It's HE who'll bring you back to me,
And meets us at our gate."

Repeat this aloud *three* times while the candle continues to burn.

Optional   Read Psalm 2, "Why do the heathen rage."

For a Safe Air Trip

Candle color   Blue

Day of the week   Thursday

Affirmation   "The God that made the birds fly,
Also made the clear Blue sky
In which my plane soars high and low
So there's really no place to go
To find Peace and Protection
For all is THY PERFECTION!"

Repeat this aloud *seven* times while the candle continues to burn.

There is no Psalm suggested.

For Travel in General

Candle color   Blue

Day of the week   Thursday

Affirmation   "You are my wheels, you are my heels,
It's you I trust throughout.
For I know when I get in trouble,
There's never a need to shout.
For you're always right here
When I need you most.
My Light, My Lord, My Heavenly Host."

Read this aloud *seven* times while the candle continues to burn.

Optional   Read Psalm 121, "I will lift up mine eyes."

To Reverse a Psychic Attack

Candle color   Blue

Day of the week   Thursday or *whenever needed*

Affirmation

"Black is Black
And White is White.
You who have come forth from
    DARKNESS
Must now become LIGHT!
What you have wished ME,
Now returns home to YOU.
For the Black that you've sent,
Has now become Blue."

Repeat this aloud *nine* times while the candle continues to burn.

Optional

Read Psalm 18, "I will love thee."

To Exorcise a Ghost or Spirit

Candle color

Violet or black

Day of the week

Saturday

Affirmation

"Be Gone . . . Be Gone,
Away You Go!
Why You Have Come,
I need not know!
By the Christ in Me
I now set you Free.
Be Gone . . . Be Gone!"

Repeat this aloud *nine* times while the candle continues to burn.

Optional

Read Psalm 40, "I waited patiently."

To Stop Gossip

Candle color

Orange or silver

Day of the week

Monday

Affirmation

"Be Still All Tongues,
    Be Still!
Be quiet all those who Will
    Speak false about me now.
May peace return to my door,
    Now and forever more.
Be Still All Tongues.
    Be Still!"

Repeat aloud *nine* times while the candle continues to burn.

Optional

Read Psalm 36, "The transgression."

So as Not to Get Involved in Something (or with Someone)

Candle color

Orange or silver

Day of the week

Monday

Affirmation

"Foolish I am. Foolish I be.
    I come to my senses,
And now I am free.
    For the flame of this candle,
      Has burned away Thee,
And the chains that would bind,
    Fall far behind,
And I see that I'm free,
    TO BE ME!"

Repeat aloud *nine* times while the candle continues to burn.

Optional

Read Psalm 56, "Be merciful unto me."

SELF-IMPROVEMENT

To Pass Examinations

Candle color

Yellow

Day of the week   Wednesday

Affirmation

"A Mind that is quick
Is mine I know.
A Mind that is sharp
Now makes me grow!
I never forget so
I remember it all.
My God gives me wisdom,
So I never fall."

Repeat this aloud *five* times while the candle
continues to burn.

Optional   Read Psalm 5, "Give ear to my words."

To Become Psychic

Candle color   White

Day of the week   Monday

Affirmation

"Astral vision I now claim,
Clairvoyance and ESP are my name.
I see, hear, and touch
Like never before.
To me all which was closed
Is an open door."

Repeat aloud *nine* times while the candle
continues to burn.

Optional   Read Psalm 23, "The Lord is my shepherd."

To Conquer Overeating

Candle color   Yellow

Day of the week   Tuesday

Affirmation   "I eat to live, not live to eat,
My Higher Power is my meat.
The hunger that I once did feel,
I now realize was not real.
I ate for reasons wrong I know,
So I break these habits
And claim MY GLOW!"

Repeat aloud *six* times while the candle continues to burn.

Optional   Repeat Psalm 69, "Save me, O God."

To Overcome Hatred

Candle color   Orange

Day of the week   Monday

Affirmation   "As One Mind . . . One Soul
    Is All that there is,
I cannot hate another.
For everywhere I throw a stone,
I'm sure to hit a Brother.
So Love is all I can give,
    Or Toss, or throw or scatter.
For anything else is sure to go
    Pitter, Patter, Splatter!"

Repeat aloud *seven* times while the candle continues to burn.

Optional   Read Psalm 137, "By the rivers of."

For Inner Peace

Candle color   Silver or white

Day of the week   Monday or *whenever needed*

Affirmation	"PEACE is the name of my River, PEACE is the name of my game. Wherever I Live, Go or Travel, HIS PEACE is always the Same. I go to the mountains, Or down to the sea, And PEACE walks by my side. I stop and close my eyes right now, And feel the PEACE inside!" Repeat aloud *seven* times while the candle continues to burn.
Optional	Read Psalm 147, "Praise ye the Lord."

To Conquer Fear

Candle color	Red or gold
Day of the week	Sunday
Affirmation	"Where love lights burn, There can't glow fear For love is all there is! With God my constant spotlight beam Perfect love is always His. I fear not, knowing love is mine. And feel His presence near. In His Light darkness flees, And in its place is Cheer." Repeat aloud *five* times while the candle continues to burn.
Optional	Read Psalm 116, "I love the Lord."

To Get Rid of Guilt Feelings

Candle color	White

Day of the week   Monday

Affirmation   "Whoever plays the Game of Life,
Plays with the cards they're dealt.
Sometimes they're GOOD,
Sometimes they're BAD.
Ofttimes they're never felt.
Whatever happened in the Past,
I can't change one iota.
But when I think about today
I can set a brand new Quota!
So I forgive myself and you as well,
And break the chains that hold me."

Repeat this aloud *two* times while the candle continues to burn.

Optional   Read Psalm 51, "Have mercy upon me."

To Create Genuine Compassion

Candle color   Blue

Day of the week   Thursday

Affirmation   "I walk a mile in your shoes
So I can know you better.
They make me tall, they make me short.
I understand your Feather!
My Love and Pity go out to you,
I feel your sorrow burden,
It's not for me to judge your life,
That's done by another Warden."

Read aloud *three* times while the candle continues to burn.

Optional   Read Psalm 32, "Blessed is he."

To Gain Self-Confidence

Candle color	Red or gold
Day of the week	Sunday
Affirmation	"Who I Am and What I Know,

"Who I Am and What I Know,
Is always known to YOU.
So never can I really fail
No matter what I do.
Whenever I think I'm all alone,
I have simply to look around
At rocks and trees and birds
   and things for
I stand on Holy Ground.
So Self-confident I AM as
   I pass through Life,
Knowing that things are always fine.
And that being alive
   is NICE!"

Read aloud *nine* times while the candle continues to burn.

Optional	Read Psalm 78, "Give ear O my people."

For Spiritual Growth

Candle color	Blue
Day of the week	Thursday
Affirmation	"My inner Self unfolds this day,

"My inner Self unfolds this day,
I feel the growth take place.
I see myself enlarge and expand,
I like what I see in my face.
My Path and Fate I understand,
And Know what I must do
To make my life work as it should,
To set my Temple true!"

97

Repeat aloud *seven* times while the candle continues to burn.

Optional   Read Psalm 14, "The fool hath said."

To Gain Physical Strength

Candle color   Green

Day of the week   Friday

Affirmation   "The STRENGTH I seek I already OWN,
                  It's here for me to use.
                  I simply have to reach right out,
                  It's there for me to choose.
                  Day by day in every way,
                  I now get stronger still.
                  I only have to open up,
                  And let come in THY WILL!"

Repeat aloud *three* times while the candle continues to burn.

No Psalm is suggested.

To Overcome Nervousness or Anxiety

Candle color   Blue

Day of the week   Thursday

Affirmation   "I now RELAX . . . I now LET GO,
                  I now LET GOD so I can GROW.
                  My fears are gone,
                  My doubts go too.
                  I feel YOUR LOVE
                  Through and through.
                  With every Breath
                  I Breathe in PEACE,
                  And know 'tis YOU
                  My Soul doth keep!"

Repeat aloud *nine* times while the candle continues to burn.

Optional   Read Psalm 91, "He that dwelleth in."

To Increase (Restore) Sexual Potency

Candle color   Red

Day of the week   Sunday

Affirmation   "A HOT young man (woman)
                  I now BE-COME.
                  Once again I climb the Tree
                  Of longing and lust and vigor
                      and new sensuality!
                  The energy of YOUTH in me,
                  Now beats within my chest.
                  The PASSION I now feel inside
                  Shall never take a rest!"

Repeat aloud *seven* times while the candle continues to burn.

Optional   Read Psalm 45, "My heart is inditing."

To Reach a Right Decision (in Any Matter)

Candle color   Blue

Day of the week   Thursday

Affirmation   "I know what I should do NOW,
                  I know not what to say.
                  I know not where to go,
                  I know not when to play.
                  But deep inside I have a Guide,
                  Who KNOWS what I should do.
                  I simply have to turn within
                  And 'Listen' to What's TRUE."

Repeat aloud *five* times while the candle continues to burn.

Optional   Read verses 137 to 144 *only* of Psalm 119, "Righteous art thou."

CREATING YOUR OWN SPELLS

The various spells presented here should in no way be assumed to be the only way in which a particular change can be brought about. I have simply presented a number of rituals for a variety of situations that are most commonly needed. Should you have a need that is *not* covered by one of these, it is perfectly okay to create your own spell. To do this succesfully, simply keep in mind exactly what it is that you wish to bring about.

First, note which color and which planet and day have rulership over the action you wish to initiate. One easy way to do this is to refer to the list of Color Keys (page 65). For example, suppose you are frequently losing your temper. If you consult this list, you will see that the color connected with temper is in the red group. This immediately tells you that you must begin your candle burning on a Sunday evening and that you should use a red candle.

You now take a piece of paper and a pen or pencil, and write a spell for yourself to use during this ritual. This spell can be of any length—as short or long as you wish. If at all possible, however, try to make it rhyme. If you can do this (it doesn't have to be fancy), you will give more magical power to the spell, for rhymes are more quickly accepted by the unconscious mind. Why this is so is not known, but it has proved true for many centuries.

Once you get the knack of creating your own spells, you may prefer them to those provided here, for they will be *your very own*.

Remember that in the very early days, before telephones and televisions, before newspapers and books, magicians and wise women always created their own magick. There was no other way.

7

Eating Color

*And the manna was as coriander seed, and the
color thereof as the color of bdellium.*

(NUMBERS 11:7)

Everything that exists may be expressed in terms of color, since
color is just another name to describe the energy or spirit from
which everything is composed.

Most persons are already familiar with the idea that everything
that exists in the Cosmos is made up of atoms and molecules.
Dinshah P. Ghadiali, whose outstanding work as a color investigator I have already alluded to, spent many years in research to
connect the then-known elements (in 1966) with the various
twelve tones of his particular color system, which he called *Spectro-
Chrome.* While all the known elements, when placed in a state of
disruption, emit a particular set of color lines known as *Fraun-
holder lines,* one particular color was found by Dinshah to
predominate.

It is this single color, then, that has been correlated with the various chemical elements and, of course, with various foods composed of them.

Following is a list of elements by single-color predominance, as determined by Dinshah and published by his son Darius in his book *Let There Be Light:*

RED
cadmium
hydrogen
krypton
neon

ORANGE
aluminum
antimony
arsenic
boron
calcium
copper
helium
selenium
silicon
xenon

YELLOW
beryllium
carbon
iridium
magnesium
molybdenum
osmium
palladium
platinum
rhenium
rhodium
ruthenium

sodium
tin
tungsten

LEMON
cerium
germanium
gold
hafnium
iodine
iron
lanthanum
neodymium
phosphorus
praseodymium
protactinium
samarium
scandium
silver
sulphur
thorium
titanium
uranium
vanadium
yttrium
zirconium

GREEN
barium
chlorine

nitrogen
radium
tellurium
thallium

TURQUOISE
chromium
fluorine
mercury
nickel
niobium
tantalum
zinc

BLUE
cesium
indium
oxygen

INDIGO
bismuth
ionium
lead
polonium

VIOLET
actinium
cobalt
gallium
radon

PURPLE
bromine
europium
gadolinium
terbium

MAGENTA
lithium
potassium
rubidium
strontium

SCARLET
argon
dysprosium
erbium
holmium
lutecium
manganese
thulium
ytterbium

Besides deriving this list, Dinshah discovered that certain colors influence specific glands in the body. Hence, one can stimulate the secretion of a specific gland by subjecting the body to a particular color. As will later be seen, this can be done in various ways, among which eating those foods that have a predominance of a particular color is perhaps the easiest.

Certainly we have all had the experience of eating a particular food only to find that it did not agree with our digestion, or perhaps actually made us ill. Why this was so may not have been known at the time. What I am suggesting is that there may be a connection between a particular color or colors we surround ourselves with and the state of our health.

Following is Dinshah's correlation of colors to glandular stimulation (a partial listing from *Let There Be Light*), which gets us thinking along some unusual lines:

COLOR	ORGAN
Red	Liver
Orange	Thyroid, lungs
Yellow	Nerves, digestive system
Lemon	Thymus
Green	Pituitary
Turquoise	Skin
Blue	Pineal
Indigo	Parathyroid
Violet	Spleen
Magenta	Heart, kidneys, reproductive system

The following correspondence between colors and vitamins is yet another discovery, this time gleaned from my own research.

Vitamin	Color
A	Magenta
B_1 (thiamine)	Turquoise
B_2 (riboflavin)	Indigo
B_6 (pyridoxine)	Orange, purple
B_{12} (cobalamin)	Purple, green
Biotin	Scarlet
Choline	Orange
Inositol	Turquoise
Folic acid	Blue
Niacin	Violet
Niacinamide	Indigo
Pantothenic acid	Violet

PABA	Turquoise
B_{15} (pangamic acid)	Purple
B complex	Magenta
C (rose hips)	Violet
(bioflavinoids)	Orange
(rutin)	Violet
D	Orange
E	Green

HOW TO DETERMINE YOUR COLOR HUNGER

Before I share with you a detailed list of various foods and their dominant color energy, I must discuss exactly how you can determine for yourself what color—or colors—you need to bring into your life. Fortunately, since we are dealing with energy here and not matter, this is not a difficult task—although it will require a visit to your local art supply or stationery store.

Go to the store and obtain a small basic box of colored crayons and a package of colored paper. It is very important that both contain at least the twelve colors I have already spoken of: red, orange, scarlet, green, yellow, blue, purple, turquoise, magenta, indigo, violet, lemon. Most likely your colored paper package will also contain black paper, and sometimes even brown. Cut 2-inch squares from each sheet of colored paper. In order to use these colors you will also have to make yourself a pendulum. Obtain a small glass (crystal) or plastic bead, or a small ring, and attach it to a piece of thread (preferably black silk or plastic fishing line). This thread must be pliant and strong.

Once you have made your pendulum, you should carry it with you in your pocket for a few days so your vibrations can enter it. At least once a day, take it out and hold it between both hands while taking three deep breaths, which you will exhale slowly. This will further charge the pendulum with your energy. Now you are ready to start using your pendulum.

Take a food that you eat and that you know is good for you. Place this food by itself on a clean plate and suspend the pendulum over it. In a few minutes you will notice that the pendulum will begin to rotate in a circle clockwise as it hangs over the food. This means that the food is good for you. Now take something you know you shouldn't eat, such as a glass of saltwater. Again, suspend your pendulum over this food. You will note that the pendulum begins to rotate in a counterclockwise motion. This means *no*.

For some people, the pendulum will move in a circle to indicate *yes,* and simply swing back and forth (oscillate) to indicate *no*. Sometimes the yes movement might simply be circular, in either direction. What you must determine is exactly how the pendulum moves for yes and no specifically for you! Once you have this knowledge, you can begin to use the pendulum for all kinds of color magick.

For instance, while holding your pendulum in your right hand, pick up with your left hand a small square you have cut from each sheet of construction paper. As you hold each color in turn, mentally ask the question "Do I need this color?" Wait for the pendulum to begin moving. Once you have got an answer, move on to the next color, and so on. Most likely only one color, or at the most two, will be indicated.

The same thing can be done by using colored crayons. To get a more accurate reading, however, you may wish to peel off any label on the crayon itself. If the label is colored, it can interfere with the results. Simply peel it off the entire crayon or cut off a piece of each crayon that does not have a label.

Once you have obtained a definite yes for a particular color, or colors, you can proceed to introduce this color into your life in various ways, including food, clothing, and room decorations.

FOODS AND COLOR VIBRATIONS

Following is a list of various foods and the colors to which they correspond, derived from my own research. While this list (which has never before appeared in print) is essentially complete, the color correspondence of many foods may surprise you. For instance, while beef appears red in color, its actual energy color is green, which no doubt accounts for its ability to nourish the body. Cashews and peanuts, which appear tan and light brown, are respectively magenta and orange. A careful study of, and meditation on, this list will reveal a great many wonderful things concerning the Divine Wisdom of the Cosmic.

Food	Color
Alfalfa	Green
Almond	Purple
American cheese	Blue
Apple	Scarlet
Apricot	Yellow
Arrowroot	Yellow
Asparagus	Purple
Avocado	Scarlet
Bacon	Red
Baking powder	Magenta
Baking soda	Lemon
Banana	Violet
Barley	Violet
Basil	Lemon
Bay leaves	Lemon
Beef	Green
Beer	Yellow
Black olives	Green
Blueberry	Purple
Bluefish	Indigo
Broccoli	Purple
Brussels sprouts	Turquoise
Buckwheat	Purple
Cabbage (red)	Red
Camembert	Blue
Cantaloupe	Indigo

Caraway seed	Violet
Cardamom seed	Indigo
Carrot	Orange
Cashew	Magenta
Cauliflower	Orange
Celery	Green
Cheddar cheese	Yellow
Cherry	Red
Chestnut	Yellow
Chicken	Orange
Chicken liver	Green
Chinese tea	Scarlet
Chocolate	Violet
Cinnamon	Purple
Cloves	Red
Coconut	Purple
Coffee	Purple
Cognac (brandy)	Orange
Cola (Coke)	Orange
Corn	Scarlet
Cornstarch	Blue
Cottage cheese	Lemon
Crab	Lemon
Cranberry	Indigo
Crème de menthe	Violet
Cucumber	Lemon
Date	Orange
Dill seed	Orange
Duck	Orange
Egg (whole)	Lemon
Eggplant	Purple
Endive	Green
Evaporated milk	Lemon
Fennel	Lemon
Fig	Turquoise
Filbert (hazelnut)	Lemon

Flounder	Orange
Garlic	Blue
Gelatin	Indigo
Ginger	Lemon
Grape (green)	Green
Grapefruit	Red
Green olive	Violet
Green pepper (bell)	Blue
Green pepper (hot)	Red
Halibut	Scarlet
Ham	Scarlet
Hashish	Indigo
Honey	Red, blue
Honeydew melon	Magenta
Lamb	Lemon
Lemon	Red
Lentil	Magenta
Lettuce (Boston)	Green
Lettuce (romaine)	Yellow
Lima bean	Magenta
Mace	Violet
Mackerel	Turquoise
Mango	Turquoise
Marjoram	Green
Milk (cow)	Orange
Mint	Blue
Molasses	Orange
Mozzarella	Purple
Muenster	Turquoise
Mushroom	Turquoise
Mustard	Purple
MSG (monosodium glutamate)	Yellow
Nectarine	Red
Nutmeg	Scarlet
Oats	Yellow
Okra	Orange

Onion (red)	Red
Orange	Orange
Oregano	Indigo, magenta
Paprika	Red
Parmesan cheese	Turquoise
Parsley	Red
Peach	Yellow, turquoise
Peanut	Orange
Pear	Green
Peas	Green
Pecan	Purple
Pepper (black)	Red
Pineapple	Yellow
Pistachio	Magenta
Poppy seed	Purple
Postum	Magenta
Potato	Indigo
Provolone	Scarlet
Pumpkin	Yellow
Radish	Blue
Red plum	Orange
Red snapper	Lemon
Rhubarb	Red
Rice (white)	Orange
Roquefort	Blue
Rosemary	Purple
Rye	Yellow
Rum (white)	Lemon
Sage	Blue
Sanka	Yellow
Salmon	Turquoise
Salt	Indigo
Sardine	Green
Sausage	Violet
Scallops	Violet
Scotch whiskey	Scarlet

Scrod	Lemon
Sesame	Lemon
Seven-Up (soda)	Blue
Sherry	Magenta
Shrimp	Red
Sole	Lemon
Southern Comfort	Yellow
Spinach	Turquoise
Sprouts (alfalfa)	Green
Sprouts (mung)	Magenta
Sprouts (wheat)	Yellow
Squash (butternut)	Orange
Squash (yellow)	Lemon
Strawberry	Scarlet
String bean	Blue
Sugar (cane)	Magenta, red
Sunflower seeds	Green
Sweet potato	Scarlet
Sweet'n Low	Scarlet
Swiss cheese	Yellow
Swordfish	Turquoise
Tab (diet soda)	Turquoise
Tapioca	Blue
Tarragon	Indigo
Tea	Scarlet
Thyme	Indigo
Tobacco	Blue
Tomato	Red
Trout (sea)	Lemon
Tuna fish	Magenta
Turkey	Red
Turnip	Blue
Tylenol	Purple
Vanilla	Blue
Veal	Indigo
Vermouth	Green

Vodka	Magenta
Walnut	Indigo
Watercress	Green
Watermelon	Indigo
Wheat bran	Purple
Wheat germ	Red
Wheat (whole)	Yellow
Whitefish	Indigo
White snapper	Yellow
Wine (red)	Purple
Wine (white)	Yellow
Yeast (baker's)	Turquoise
Yeast (brewer's)	Orange
Yellow wax bean	Orange
Yogurt	Scarlet

While it was my original intent to make this list as complete as possible, one food seemed ever to defy my analysis. This food was pork. It was as if the nature of pork contained a plethora of indistinguishable colors having no definite patterns. Perhaps this was the basis for the ancient prohibition against eating the flesh of this animal. It was also of great interest to find honey expressed as both red and blue. Certainly this source of almost instant energy both soothes and stimulates at the same time.

Take a few moments to look over this list, seeking out those foods you eat on a regular basis. You may be surprised to see that you have been drawn to select foods corresponding to a certain color or colors. Likewise, you may find that foods that appear to disagree with you—producing indigestion, rashes, etc.—also fall into certain color groups. There is a reason for everything that you eat and everything that you don't!

Later on we will investigate the connection between the time of day we do certain things, including eating, and color. For instance, if you always arise at the same time each day and eat the same food for breakfast, don't be surprised that when you change the time of your breakfast, you also change the food eaten!

This is the magical and mystical side of color. The problem is that we do not normally think about these things. Rather, we simply do them. As we begin to consciously tune into the magical color connection, we begin to truly see things, not just look at them. In other words, through a true perception of color, we become aware of God's plan for both the world and ourselves.

Now let's go back to the use of the pendulum for a moment. Suppose you have found yourself "hungry" for the color orange. This would most likely occur when someone is lacking in vitality, possibly when the person is overweight, sluggish, and lacking in ambition and especially self-confidence. That person would benefit from foods that correlate with this color. Milk, molasses, dates, red plums, and oranges are just a few such foods.

Actually wearing the color orange—blouse, dress, scarf, or even hair ribbons—would bring this color into your auric field. You may also wish to begin decorating with this color, but remember that a little orange goes a long way. Here, for instance, the right use of orange-colored pillows, curtains, or desk accessories can be a Godsend!

If you continually wake up exhausted, try going to sleep with orange ribbons tied around both wrists and, if need be, the ankles. If you do this and find yourself too energetic, however, start reducing the ribbons, one wrist or ankle at a time, until you find the correct balance.

Color is not dead. There is not color *and* something. There is only color *as* something. Similarly, there is not God and mankind, but rather only God as Man! These are very profound mysteries we learn once we begin to think, live, and breathe color.

Don't forget the connection between color and vitamin supplements. If you are lacking in a particular color energy, try taking the vitamin supplement that corresponds to this. Be sure, however, that before taking any supplements, you discuss this with your primary health-care practitioner. While vitamins are useful, they are not meant for all persons all the time.

Another way of looking at colors is in terms of their opposites. The following chart may be helpful to this kind of analysis:

Red—Blue
Orange—Indigo
Yellow—Violet
Lemon—Turquoise
Purple—Scarlet
Green—Magenta

Dinshah maintained that green and magenta were not actually opposites at all, but only appeared so. He held that green was the median color of the spectrum, and as such actually governed the "physical, positive" polarity. Magenta, on the other hand, was said to be the "emotional, negative polarity."

The relationship between lemon and turquoise is also unusual, since each contains the color green. It was Dinshah's belief that both these colors play a significant role in restoring lost health: lemon in chronic cases and turquoise in acute cases.

Thus, if you find yourself hungry for a particular color through your pendulum testing, likewise you may find yourself allergic to those foods whose color is opposite what you need. (Of course, when one speaks of allergies, remember that very often we crave those foods we are allergic to. Sugar is certainly a primary example of this.)

For example, suppose you use your pendulum as directed and find yourself in need of the color orange. Indigo is the opposite color. This means that you may actually find yourself sensitive or allergic to those foodstuffs governed by this color. For instance, indigo rules gelatin, which is the substance used in many vitamin capsules. This would mean that if you have a need for orange and you take vitamins, you may be sensitive to any vitamins in gelatin capsules!

How can you find out for sure if this is true? Use your pendulum to test the vitamins, one by one, in the same way you test for colors!

If you still have a need for a particular vitamin, but are sensitive to it owing to its packaging in gelatin, see if it is manufactured in tablet rather than capsule form.

8

Other Ways to Get the Color You Need

* * * * * *

And I saw as the color of amber, as the appearance of fire round about within it, from the appearance of his loins even upward, and from the appearance of his loins even downward, I saw as it were the appearance of fire, and it had brightness round about.

(EZEKIEL 1:27)

One way in which to change the color energy in your system is to eat it through the use of various foods or food supplements, as mentioned in Chapter 7. Still another way is to wear the color needed by changing your wardrobe altogether, or by deliberately wearing one color in preference to another. Then, of course, you can paint a room a particular color or change decorations to produce a particular effect. The goal, then, is simply to change your color energy. Once this is done, your life is bound to change accordingly.

COLOR PROJECTION

Of the many traditional methods used to change one's color, the projection of colored light on various parts of the body is one of the most ancient and widely accepted. Initially this was done with tinted windows, through which sunlight flowed. Stained glass church windows are a classic example. In these days of artificial lighting and urban dwelling, however, one may have to use electrically generated colored lights to get the same effects.

The least expensive way to do this is to obtain an old-fashioned gooseneck lamp and various colored bulbs. Often both items can be bought at a local hardware store or general merchandise store. It is usually quite easy to obtain colored bulbs for the primary colors red, yellow, blue, and green. Since bulbs in other colors are sometimes more difficult to obtain, Appendix B contains a list of suppliers.

Still another way to generate colors is with a color projector, which requires colored slides of glass or plastic to produce the different tones. Such projectors can be obtained from various sources, such as the Bruce Copen Laboratories (see Appendix B), or you may wish to create your own.

While I have a number of projectors on hand, the one I use most often is a small theater projector. I have fitted it with plastic filters manufactured by Rosco Laboratories, following the suggestions of Dinshah as to how to produce the various tones he discovered in his research. In Appendix B I have given the name and address of a source where you can obtain such a color projector as well as the filters needed.

The original Spectro-Chrome Projector manufactured by Dinshah used a combination of five monochrome glass slides to produce the twelve colors. When Dinshah ceased manufacturing these projectors, he sought to obtain less expensive plastic filters to reproduce these basic tones. Following is a chart of the original Spectro-Chrome color and the corresponding plastic number as manufactured by Rosco.

Spectro-Chrome Color	Rosco Plastic Number
Red	#818 and #828
Orange	#809 and #828
Yellow	#809
Lemon	#871 and #809
Green	#871
Turquoise	#871 and #861
Blue	#866
Indigo	#818, #859, and #861
Violet	#832, #866, and #859
Purple	#832 and #866
Magenta	#818, #828, and #866
Scarlet	#818, #810, and #861

The filter numbers may be changed from time to time, so it would be prudent to contact Dinshah Health Society (as listed in Appendix B) for an updated list. These filters can be cut into the proper size to fit the slide holder of the miniature theater projector, or any other projector you may wish to use. In the case of the colors indigo, violet, magenta, and scarlet, three plastic filters must be combined in a single slide holder to produce a particular shade of color.

A word of warning: If you are thinking of using a 35 millimeter slide projector as your light source, you *cannot* use the suggested Rosco filters internally, as you would normal slides. They will melt inside the projector and possibly catch fire. They can be mounted only outside the projector at the end of the lens, which is the way they are normally used in theater projectors.

Once you have obtained your projector and put together the various slides, you are ready. Mark the name of the color on each slide holder with a marking pen or on a file folder label. This is important, as the filters of many colors look the same before they are projected!

Assuming that you have determined what color is needed, you

can either darken your room and actually "project" that color on yourself, or you can transfer the color to another medium. If you elect the latter, you might wish to first experiment by transferring the color to ordinary drinking water. Fill a glass with pure spring water and place it directly in front of your projector lens for about ten minutes. The room should be darkened. The projector should be placed a foot or so away from the glass of water. After ten minutes, you may notice the presence of bubbles in the water, indicating that it has been charged or "potentized." You may not get these bubbles every time, however, so even if they do not appear, assume that the transfer of energy has taken place. If you wish, now place this water in a closed container from which you can take a sip periodically. It is not necessary for you to refrigerate it. Some persons prefer to place this potentized water in a sterile dropper bottle, from which they take three drops under the tongue throughout the day.

If you intend to keep your potentized water for some time, add a few drops of cognac or brandy as a preservative. If you do not do this, and the tip of the dropper accidentally touches the tongue, your solution may become contaminated. If you have chosen not to use brandy or cognac, simply squeeze the three drops onto a spoon, from which you can sip.

Still another way to transfer color energy is to use homeopathic sac lac (sugar of milk) tablets, which can be obtained at any homeopathic pharmacy. These are the so-called placebo tablets used in the manufacture of homeopathic remedies, which are exposed to the tinctures of herbs and the like. These tablets can be spread out in a shallow dish and exposed to the projected color as directed. Once potentized in this way, they can be stored in a box or vial and will remain active for an indefinite time as long as they are not exposed to any magnetic fields or strong odors, such as perfume or camphor. Many persons interested in color prefer these tablets, since they can prepare all the colors in advance, and have them on hand when needed.

The important thing is to surround yourself with the color or colors that will bring about the changes you wish in your life. If these changes should come quickly, you may elect to combine various means to bring this about.

First, you might change your wardrobe to include the color or colors you need. Second, you might add these colors to your decor. Third, you might start introducing into your diet those foods vibrating to that color. Fourth, you might bring that color into your system, either through spring water or sac lac or by projecting the color on yourself using your color projector!

For example, Mary had been struggling with a lack of prosperity in her life. By using her pendulum, she determined that she needed the color orange. She purchased orange candles and began to work the suggested candle magick to bring about a desired change in her affairs. Then she began to wear the color orange somewhere on her person every day. She added orange foods to her diet, such as carrots, cauliflower, and chicken. In addition, she obtained some orange throw pillows and placed them on the sofa and chair, where she usually sits when she returns home from work. Lastly, she has begun to use an orange light bulb or an orange color filter to project this color onto herself when relaxing in front of the television in the evening. In other words, Mary has saturated herself with orange, and, in so doing, is calling upon its magick to bring about the changes she wishes in her life.

COLOR TONES AND BREATHING

Besides these techniques, there are two additional, lesser known ways in which color can be added: sound and breath.

By now you may have reached the conclusion that all color is simply vibration. Thus it is not surprising that each corresponds to a particular musical note, which can be sounded or chanted, much like a mantra, to generate a particular hue.

Color	Musical Note and Frequency
Red	G-392
Scarlet	G-392 and D-587
Yellow	A#-466

Green	C-523
Orange	A-440
Turquoise	C#-554
Blue	D-587
Purple	A#-466 and E-659
Violet	E-659
Magenta	G-392 and E-659
Indigo	D#-622
Lemon	B-494

The cycles per second after each note can help you identify where it appears on a given musical instrument. Also note that, in some cases, two musical notes must be sounded together to produce a particular color.

On a more practical basis, with your eyes closed, you can simply hum a particular tone while mentally visualizing (picturing in the mind) a particular color. For those inclined to Oriental mantras, the sound *OM* (pronounced like the word *home*) is good to use. This is hummed at the pitch corresponding to the particular color you are seeking to generate. For example, if the color red is needed, the *OM* would be hummed on the G note while the color red is visualized.

Another way to generate color is by breathing it. This is done by mentally picturing a particular color being drawn into one's self with the incoming breath. For those who may have difficulty visualizing the various colors, the color projector is a great aid. Simply project the required color on the forehead while breathing. If this is done a few times, you can usually dispense with the projector and rely on your recall of a particular color.

The advantage of both color toning and breathing is that either exercise can be done at odd moments throughout the day without special equipment. For instance, let us assume that you are at work and have just received some disturbing news and wish to calm yourself down. Since blues and greens are the colors of peace, you can take a few moments to mentally picture these colors being drawn into yourself with each breath. As your breathing slows down with each color breath, you will feel yourself becoming calmer and calmer, less and less nervous.

Similarly, while out walking you can begin to tone a particular color as you stroll along. If you have trouble recalling the appropriate pitch, you may wish to buy an inexpensive pitchpipe at a local music store. Sounding a note on this pipe, which you can carry in your coat pocket or handbag, will enable you to do this exercise whenever you can.

The regular practice of these simple exercises will greatly increase your color magick abilities.

9

Planetary Hours and Color

When I bring you coloured toys, my child, I understand why there is such a play of colours on clouds, on water, and why flowers are painted in tints.

RABINDRANATH TAGORE, *The Crescent Moon* (1913)

While it is commonplace to find in most books on astrology a comparison of the various signs of the Zodiac to determine one's romantic compatibility with another, such ancient magical techniques as the Kabalah and numerology have remained the exclusive property of astrologers, including yours truly, Zolar.

Surely there is no more convincing evidence of the general belief in astrology worldwide than the traditional naming of the days of the week after the planets, the assignment of planetary hours under each, and their color correspondences. In fact, in every civilized nation, the days of the week are named after planets. Certainly, it is not a mere accident or chance that this time-honored tradition has persisted. For most of us, however, how to understand and use the planetary hours has long since been forgotten.

Not only is there general agreement as to the names of the days and their planetary correspondence, but astrological records traced back as far as 27 B.C. agree on the assignment and order of planetary hours for any given day (which begins at sunrise) and is ruled by that planet which rules the day itself. On Sunday the first hour after sunrise is ruled by the Sun. On Monday, the first hour is ruled by the Moon, and so on. But while the origin of this planetary assignment remains unknown, the mythological meaning of the days is quite certain.

Sunday (color red) is derived from an Anglo-Saxon word *Sunan daeg,* and yet earlier no doubt from the Roman *Dies solis,* the "day of the Sun." The worship of the Sun as a god can be traced back to many ancient civilizations, especially the Egyptians. And of course, Sunday has become the traditional day of worship for Christians, by whom Christ is held as the "Light of the World."

Monday (color orange) is also derived from an Anglo-Saxon word, *Monan daeg* or "Moon's day." The ancient Romans had called this day *Dies lunae,* while the French still call it *Lundi.* For the ancient Greeks, this was their day for rest and worship.

Tuesday (color yellow) is derived from *Tirsdag, Tir,* or *Tyr,* which is the name of the Norse god of war, called Tiw by the Anglo-Saxons. The Romans called this same day *Dies Martis.* The French call it *Mardi,* which clearly connects it with Mars, the God of War. To this day, residents of New Orleans celebrate Fat Tuesday, or Mardi Gras, the day before Ash Wednesday. Originally a fat bull, decorated with garlands of roses, was led through the streets eventually to be slaughtered and barbecued. Clearly this relic comes to us from ancient Egypt, or even greater antiquity.

Wednesday (color green) comes from the Scandinavian *Wotan,* or once again, *Woten's daeg.* Woden, known also as the Norse god Odin, is the selfsame god who gave us the Runes, which have only recently returned to their proper position as a system of divination. The French name for the day is *Mercredi,* while the

Roman is *Mercoledi*. Here Mercury, the messenger of the gods, rules and is identified with Odin, bringer of wisdom and poetry, as well as the Greek god Hermes.

Thursday (color blue) or *Thor's daeg,* received its name from Thor, the Scandinavian god of thunder. He was the son of Odin and rode in a chariot driven by goats; he carried a hammer—a thunderbolt—which was returned after it had been cast. The Romans called this same god Jupiter and his day, *Dies Jovis* (after Jupiter or Jove). The French call the day *Jeudi* or *Jeu* (piter's) day.

Friday (color indigo) gets its name from Frigga, Odin's wife, whom the Romans called Venus. The French still call it *Vendredi*. Among some folks, this day is considered unlucky, possibly based on the belief that it was the day on which Jesus was crucified. It was also the day on which Adam was created, according to the Bible, as well as the day on which Christopher Columbus reached America.

Saturday (color violet or black) is, of course, Saturn's day. This is the day on which God rested after creating the world, hence the Jewish Sabbath tradition. Interestingly, Saturn is also identified with the Greek god Chronos, god of time. This is why Saturn is often characterized at New Year's as Father Time, carrying a sickle—to dispense Karma, no doubt.

The English names for the days of the week for the most part were derived from Saxon names, which in turn were derived from the Scandinavians and Romans, who occupied England in early times. The French, Spanish, and Italian names were also derived from their Roman ancestors. But is it not unusual that in many cases the names are the same?

In India, the Buddhists of long ago chose to name and divide their week in exactly the same manner. Hiru, the Hindu name for the Sun, rules Sunday; Kandu, the Hindu name for the Moon, rules Monday; Angahru (Mars) rules Tuesday; Badahu (Mercury) rules Wednesday; Brihaspati (Jupiter) rules Thursday; Sicura (Venus) rules Friday, and Henaharu (Saturn) rules Saturday. Surely there must have existed a general knowledge of astronomy to cause all ancient civilizations to divide the week into seven days and to name each day after a principal deity whose counterpart can be found in every other civilization.

To summarize:

Day of the Week	Planet Ruling	Color	Day of Worship for
Sunday	Sun	Red	Christians
Monday	Moon	Orange	Greeks
Tuesday	Mars	Yellow	Persians
Wednesday	Mercury	Green	Assyrians
Thursday	Jupiter	Blue	Egyptians
Friday	Venus	Indigo	Islamics
Saturday	Saturn	Violet	Jews

Of course, when I refer to the day of worship, I mean the ancient religions found in each nation before the influence of Christianity.

PLANETARY HOURS—YET ANOTHER BELIEF

Not only did the ancient astrologers and Magi believe that each day was ruled by a particular planet, but they believed that each hour was under a particular planetary rulership.

Each planetary day of twenty-four hours was divided into two periods: sunrise to sunset and sunset to sunrise. The actual time from sunrise to sunset was itself divided by twelve, yielding twelve unequal hours, each assigned in turn to a particular planet's influence, commencing with that planet ruling the day and following a specific sequence that had been recorded in ancient times. While the origin of this planetary sequence is unknown, a work entitled the *Oedipus Aegypticus,* published in 1642 by Athanacius Kircher, contains at least three examples of ancient engravings, which though from different times and sources, contain the exact same hourly assignments. In all three engravings, the planets are arranged in the sequence Saturn, Jupiter, Mars, Sun, Venus, Mercury, and the Moon. (Astute readers will note, if they have not already done so, that the planets Uranus, Neptune, and Pluto— discovered at a much later date—have been omitted. It may be argued that the ancients did not know of these planets; or that if they were known, their influence might have been believed to be on higher planes—spiritual or psychic—and that therefore they were omitted with good intention.) Thus, the planetary hour system for each day begins at sunrise, with the planet for that particular day ruling the first planetary hour. Hence, on Saturday, the first planetary hour is ruled by Saturn; on Sunday, the first hour is ruled by the Sun; on Monday, the first hour is ruled by the Moon, and so on.

Using Saturday (ruled by Saturn) as an example, we find the following:

Hour of Day	Ruling Planet	Hour of Day	Ruling Planet
1st*	Saturn (violet)	13th	Mercury (green)
2nd	Jupiter (blue)	14th	Moon (orange)
3rd	Mars (yellow)	15th*	Saturn (violet)
4th	Sun (red)	16th	Jupiter (blue)
5th	Venus (indigo)	17th	Mars (yellow)
6th	Mercury (green)	18th	Sun (red)
7th	Moon (orange)	19th	Venus (indigo)
8th*	Saturn (violet)	20th	Mercury (green)
9th	Jupiter (blue)	21st	Moon (orange)
10th	Mars (yellow)	22nd*	Saturn (violet)
11th	Sun (red)	23rd	Jupiter (blue)
12th	Venus (indigo)	24th	Mars (yellow)

*Marks start of each planetary cycle.

In other words, the planet ruling a particular day rules the first, eighth, fifteenth, and twenty-second hour of that day. Remember, too, that in the planetary hour system each day begins at sunrise and ends at sunrise the next day, whereas our calendar day begins at midnight and ends at midnight the next day. Hence, any time before sunrise belongs to the night hours of the day before.

To make this point clear, here's an example. If sunrise on Saturday takes place at 5:04 A.M. and you wish to know what planet rules at 4:45 A.M. (before sunrise), you must look to the chart for the previous day, which in this case would be Friday, not Saturday.

HOW YOU CAN USE PLANETARY HOURS

Let us see how the planetary hours can tell us the nature of the color magick at work at a particular moment in time.

One of the most insightful uses of this esoteric knowledge is in determining whether or not someone is really our Soul Mate. A Soul Mate is someone with whom we have a special destiny and karmic relationship. He or she can be a lover, a husband or wife, a son or daughter, even a parent. A Soul Mate can also be a special friend with whom we have an understanding or a knowing that transcends time and space. Often we have ESP with our Soul Mate.

To determine whether or not you are a Soul Mate with another, you need to know the same things an astrologer would require in order to cast an accurate horoscope: the time (A.M. or P.M.) of birth, the date of birth (day and year), and the place of birth (city and state). Remember, too, that arriving at the correct time of birth may require deducting an hour for Daylight Savings Time, should you or your partner have been born during the summer months or during World War II. This information can be obtained from any good almanac or sometimes from the city hall in the town of your birth. As for the place of birth, be concerned here only with the latitude of the birthplace. This can be obtained by looking at any good map.

Below you will find six tables showing planetary hours and sunrise times for various months for both north and south latitude. *North latitude* means being born above the equator. *South latitude* means being born below the equator.

PLANETARY HOUR TABLE 1
December and January, North Latitude
June and July, South Latitude

S	M	T	W	TH	F	S	25–35	35–45	45–55
			SUNRISE					AM	
Sun	Moon	Mars	Merc	Jup	Ven	Sat	6:58	7:25	8:05
Ven	Sat	Sun	Moon	Mars	Merc	Jup	7:48	8:10	8:45
Merc	Jup	Ven	Sat	Sun	Moon	Mars	8:38	8:56	9:24
Moon	Mars	Merc	Jup	Ven	Sat	Sun	9:29	9:43	10:03
Sat	Sun	Moon	Mars	Merc	Jup	Ven	10:19	10:28	10:42
Jup	Ven	Sat	Sun	Moon	Mars	Merc	11:10	11:14	11:21
			NOON					PM	
Mars	Merc	Jup	Ven	Sat	Sun	Moon	0:00	0:00	0:00
Sun	Moon	Mars	Merc	Jup	Ven	Sat	0:50	0:46	0:39
Ven	Sat	Sun	Moon	Mars	Merc	Jup	1:41	1:32	1:18
Merc	Jup	Ven	Sat	Sun	Moon	Mars	2:31	2:18	1:57
Moon	Mars	Merc	Jup	Ven	Sat	Sun	3:22	3:04	2:36
Sat	Sun	Moon	Mars	Merc	Jup	Ven	4:12	3:50	3:15
			SUNSET					PM	
Jup	Ven	Sat	Sun	Moon	Mars	Merc	5:02	4:35	3:55
Mars	Merc	Jup	Ven	Sat	Sun	Moon	6:12	5:50	5:15
Sun	Moon	Mars	Merc	Jup	Ven	Sat	7:22	7:04	6:36
Ven	Sat	Sun	Moon	Mars	Merc	Jup	8:31	8:18	7:57
Merc	Jup	Ven	Sat	Sun	Moon	Mars	9:41	9:32	9:18
Moon	Mars	Merc	Jup	Ven	Sat	Sun	10:50	10:46	10:39
			MIDNIGHT					AM	
Sat	Sun	Moon	Mars	Merc	Jup	Ven	0:00	0:00	0:00
Jup	Ven	Sat	Sun	Moon	Mars	Merc	1:10	1:14	1:21
Mars	Merc	Jup	Ven	Sat	Sun	Moon	2:19	2:28	2:42
Sun	Moon	Mars	Merc	Jup	Ven	Sat	3:29	3:42	4:03
Ven	Sat	Sun	Moon	Mars	Merc	Jup	4:38	4:56	5:24
Merc	Jup	Ven	Sat	Sun	Moon	Mars	4:48	5:10	6:45

PLANETARY HOUR TABLE 2
November and February, North Latitude
May and August, South Latitude

S	M	T	W	TH	F	S	25–35	35–45	45–55
			SUNRISE					AM	
Sun	Moon	Mars	Merc	Jup	Ven	Sat	6:38	6:56	7:20
Ven	Sat	Sun	Moon	Mars	Merc	Jup	7:31	7:46	8:07
Merc	Jup	Ven	Sat	Sun	Moon	Mars	8:25	8:37	8:54
Moon	Mars	Merc	Jup	Ven	Sat	Sun	9:19	9:28	9:40
Sat	Sun	Moon	Mars	Merc	Jup	Ven	10:12	10:18	10:27
Jup	Ven	Sat	Sun	Moon	Mars	Merc	11:07	11:09	11:13
			NOON					PM	
Mars	Merc	Jup	Ven	Sat	Sun	Moon	0:00	0:00	0:00
Sun	Moon	Mars	Merc	Jup	Ven	Sat	0:54	0:51	0:47
Ven	Sat	Sun	Moon	Mars	Merc	Jup	1:48	1:42	1:34
Merc	Jup	Ven	Sat	Sun	Moon	Mars	2:42	2:32	2:20
Moon	Mars	Merc	Jup	Ven	Sat	Sun	3:35	3:23	3:06
Sat	Sun	Moon	Mars	Merc	Jup	Ven	4:29	4:14	3:53
			SUNSET					PM	
Jup	Ven	Sat	Sun	Moon	Mars	Merc	5:22	5:04	4:40
Mars	Merc	Jup	Ven	Sat	Sun	Moon	6:29	6:14	5:53
Sun	Moon	Mars	Merc	Jup	Ven	Sat	7:35	7:23	7:06
Ven	Sat	Sun	Moon	Mars	Merc	Jup	8:42	8:32	8:20
Merc	Jup	Ven	Sat	Sun	Moon	Mars	9:48	9:42	9:34
Moon	Mars	Merc	Jup	Ven	Sat	Sun	10:54	10:51	10:47
			MIDNIGHT					AM	
Sat	Sun	Moon	Mars	Merc	Jup	Ven	0:00	0:00	0:00
Jup	Ven	Sat	Sun	Moon	Mars	Merc	1:06	1:09	1:13
Mars	Merc	Jup	Ven	Sat	Sun	Moon	2:12	2:18	2:27
Sun	Moon	Mars	Merc	Jup	Ven	Sat	3:19	3:28	3:40
Ven	Sat	Sun	Moon	Mars	Merc	Jup	4:25	4:37	4:54
Merc	Jup	Ven	Sat	Sun	Moon	Mars	5:31	5:46	6:07

PLANETARY HOUR TABLE 3
October and March, North Latitude
April and September, South Latitude

S	M	T	W	TH	F	S	25–35	35–45	45–55
								AM	
			SUNRISE						
Sun	Moon	Mars	Merc	Jup	Ven	Sat	6:19	6:27	6:39
Ven	Sat	Sun	Moon	Mars	Merc	Jup	7:15	7:22	7:32
Merc	Jup	Ven	Sat	Sun	Moon	Mars	8:12	8:18	8:26
Moon	Mars	Merc	Jup	Ven	Sat	Sun	9:09	9:13	9:19
Sat	Sun	Moon	Mars	Merc	Jup	Ven	10:06	10:09	10:13
Jup	Ven	Sat	Sun	Moon	Mars	Merc	11:03	11:04	11:06
			NOON					**PM**	
Mars	Merc	Jup	Ven	Sat	Sun	Moon	0:00	0:00	0:00
Sun	Moon	Mars	Merc	Jup	Ven	Sat	0:57	0:56	0:54
Ven	Sat	Sun	Moon	Mars	Merc	Jup	1:54	1:51	1:47
Merc	Jup	Ven	Sat	Sun	Moon	Mars	2:51	2:47	2:41
Moon	Mars	Merc	Jup	Ven	Sat	Sun	3:48	3:42	3:34
Sat	Sun	Moon	Mars	Merc	Jup	Ven	4:45	4:38	4:28
			SUNSET					**PM**	
Jup	Ven	Sat	Sun	Moon	Mars	Merc	5:41	5:33	5:21
Mars	Merc	Jup	Ven	Sat	Sun	Moon	6:45	6:38	6:28
Sun	Moon	Mars	Merc	Jup	Ven	Sat	7:48	7:42	7:34
Ven	Sat	Sun	Moon	Mars	Merc	Jup	8:51	8:47	8:41
Merc	Jup	Ven	Sat	Sun	Moon	Mars	9:54	9:51	9:47
Moon	Mars	Merc	Jup	Ven	Sat	Sun	10:57	10:56	10:54
			MIDNIGHT					**AM**	
Sat	Sun	Moon	Mars	Merc	Jup	Ven	0:00	0:00	0:00
Jup	Ven	Sat	Sun	Moon	Mars	Merc	1:03	1:04	1:06
Mars	Merc	Jup	Ven	Sat	Sun	Moon	2:06	2:09	2:13
Sun	Moon	Mars	Merc	Jup	Ven	Sat	3:09	3:13	3:19
Ven	Sat	Sun	Moon	Mars	Merc	Jup	4:12	4:18	4:26
Merc	Jup	Ven	Sat	Sun	Moon	Mars	5:15	5:22	5:32

PLANETARY HOUR TABLE 4
April and September, North Latitude
October and March, South Latitude

S	M	T	W	TH	F	S	25–35	35–45	45–55
			SUNRISE					AM	
Sun	Moon	Mars	Merc	Jup	Ven	Sat	5:41	5:33	5:21
Ven	Sat	Sun	Moon	Mars	Merc	Jup	6:45	6:38	6:28
Merc	Jup	Ven	Sat	Sun	Moon	Mars	7:48	7:42	7:34
Moon	Mars	Merc	Jup	Ven	Sat	Sun	8:51	8:47	8:41
Sat	Sun	Moon	Mars	Merc	Jup	Ven	9:54	9:51	9:47
Jup	Ven	Sat	Sun	Moon	Mars	Merc	10:57	10:56	10:54
			NOON					PM	
Mars	Merc	Jup	Ven	Sat	Sun	Moon	0:00	0:00	0:00
Sun	Moon	Mars	Merc	Jup	Ven	Sat	1:03	1:04	1:06
Ven	Sat	Sun	Moon	Mars	Merc	Jup	2:06	2:09	2:13
Merc	Jup	Ven	Sat	Sun	Moon	Mars	3:09	3:13	3:19
Moon	Mars	Merc	Jup	Ven	Sat	Sun	4:12	4:18	4:26
Sat	Sun	Moon	Mars	Merc	Jup	Ven	5:15	5:22	5:32
			SUNSET					PM	
Jup	Ven	Sat	Sun	Moon	Mars	Merc	6:19	6:27	6:39
Mars	Merc	Jup	Ven	Sat	Sun	Moon	7:15	7:22	7:32
Sun	Moon	Mars	Merc	Jup	Ven	Sat	8:12	8:18	8:26
Ven	Sat	Sun	Moon	Mars	Merc	Jup	9:09	9:13	9:19
Merc	Jup	Ven	Sat	Sun	Moon	Mars	10:06	10:09	10:13
Moon	Mars	Merc	Jup	Ven	Sat	Sun	11:03	11:04	11:06
			MIDNIGHT					AM	
Sat	Sun	Moon	Mars	Merc	Jup	Ven	0:00	0:00	0:00
Jup	Ven	Sat	Sun	Moon	Mars	Merc	0:57	0:56	0:54
Mars	Merc	Jup	Ven	Sat	Sun	Moon	1:54	1:51	1:47
Sun	Moon	Mars	Merc	Jup	Ven	Sat	2:51	2:47	2:41
Ven	Sat	Sun	Moon	Mars	Merc	Jup	3:48	3:42	3:34
Merc	Jup	Ven	Sat	Sun	Moon	Mars	4:45	4:38	4:28

PLANETARY HOUR TABLE 5
May and August, North Latitude
November and February, South Latitude

S	M	T	W	TH	F	S	25–35	35–45	45–55
			SUNRISE					AM	
Sun	Moon	Mars	Merc	Jup	Ven	Sat	5:22	5:04	4:40
Ven	Sat	Sun	Moon	Mars	Merc	Jup	6:29	6:14	5:53
Merc	Jup	Ven	Sat	Sun	Moon	Mars	7:35	7:23	7:06
Moon	Mars	Merc	Jup	Ven	Sat	Sun	8:42	8:32	8:20
Sat	Sun	Moon	Mars	Merc	Jup	Ven	9:48	9:42	9:34
Jup	Ven	Sat	Sun	Moon	Mars	Merc	10:54	10:51	10:47
			NOON					PM	
Mars	Merc	Jup	Ven	Sat	Sun	Moon	0:00	0:00	0:00
Sun	Moon	Mars	Merc	Jup	Ven	Sat	1:06	1:09	1:13
Ven	Sat	Sun	Moon	Mars	Merc	Jup	2:12	2:18	2:27
Merc	Jup	Ven	Sat	Sun	Moon	Mars	3:19	3:28	3:40
Moon	Mars	Merc	Jup	Ven	Sat	Sun	4:25	4:37	4:54
Sat	Sun	Moon	Mars	Merc	Jup	Ven	5:31	5:46	6:07
			SUNSET					PM	
Jup	Ven	Sat	Sun	Moon	Mars	Merc	6:38	6:56	7:20
Mars	Merc	Jup	Ven	Sat	Sun	Moon	7:31	7:46	8:07
Sun	Moon	Mars	Merc	Jup	Ven	Sat	8:25	8:37	8:54
Ven	Sat	Sun	Moon	Mars	Merc	Jup	9:19	9:28	9:40
Merc	Jup	Ven	Sat	Sun	Moon	Mars	10:12	10:18	10:27
Moon	Mars	Merc	Jup	Ven	Sat	Sun	11:07	11:09	11:13
			MIDNIGHT					AM	
Sat	Sun	Moon	Mars	Merc	Jup	Ven	0:00	0:00	0:00
Jup	Ven	Sat	Sun	Moon	Mars	Merc	0:54	0:51	0:47
Mars	Merc	Jup	Ven	Sat	Sun	Moon	1:48	1:42	1:34
Sun	Moon	Mars	Merc	Jup	Ven	Sat	2:42	2:32	2:20
Ven	Sat	Sun	Moon	Mars	Merc	Jup	3:35	3:23	3:06
Merc	Jup	Ven	Sat	Sun	Moon	Mars	4:29	4:14	3:53

PLANETARY HOUR TABLE 6
June and July, North Latitude
December and January, South Latitude

S	M	T	W	TH	F	S	25–35	35–45	45–55
			SUNRISE					AM	
Sun	Moon	Mars	Merc	Jup	Ven	Sat	5:02	4:35	3:55
Ven	Sat	Sun	Moon	Mars	Merc	Jup	6:12	5:50	5:15
Merc	Jup	Ven	Sat	Sun	Moon	Mars	7:22	7:04	6:36
Moon	Mars	Merc	Jup	Ven	Sat	Sun	8:31	8:18	7:57
Sat	Sun	Moon	Mars	Merc	Jup	Ven	9:41	9:32	9:18
Jup	Ven	Sat	Sun	Moon	Mars	Merc	10:50	10:46	10:39
			NOON					PM	
Mars	Merc	Jup	Ven	Sat	Sun	Moon	0:00	0:00	0:00
Sun	Moon	Mars	Merc	Jup	Ven	Sat	1:10	1:14	1:21
Ven	Sat	Sun	Moon	Mars	Merc	Jup	2:19	2:28	2:42
Merc	Jup	Ven	Sat	Sun	Moon	Mars	3:29	3:42	4:03
Moon	Mars	Merc	Jup	Ven	Sat	Sun	4:38	4:56	5:24
Sat	Sun	Moon	Mars	Merc	Jup	Ven	5:48	6:10	6:45
			SUNSET					PM	
Jup	Ven	Sat	Sun	Moon	Mars	Merc	6:58	7:25	8:05
Mars	Merc	Jup	Ven	Sat	Sun	Moon	7:48	8:10	8:45
Sun	Moon	Mars	Merc	Jup	Ven	Sat	8:38	8:56	9:24
Ven	Sat	Sun	Moon	Mars	Merc	Jup	9:29	9:42	10:03
Merc	Jup	Ven	Sat	Sun	Moon	Mars	10:19	10:28	10:42
Moon	Mars	Merc	Jup	Ven	Sat	Sun	11:10	11:14	11:21
			MIDNIGHT					AM	
Sat	Sun	Moon	Mars	Merc	Jup	Ven	0:00	0:00	0:00
Jup	Ven	Sat	Sun	Moon	Mars	Merc	0:50	0:46	0:39
Mars	Merc	Jup	Ven	Sat	Sun	Moon	1:41	1:32	1:18
Sun	Moon	Mars	Merc	Jup	Ven	Sat	2:31	2:18	1:57
Ven	Sat	Sun	Moon	Mars	Merc	Jup	3:22	3:04	2:36
Merc	Jup	Ven	Sat	Sun	Moon	Mars	4:12	3:50	3:15

Let us assume you were born on Thursday, October 5, 1950, at 1:40 P.M. in New York City. The latitude of New York City is 40°45′ north. Turning to Table 3, which is to be used for October and March, in north latitude, you turn to the column headed "35–45" and run your finger down to the time "1:51 P.M.," which is the first planetary hour after your birth time. You then move your finger upward to "0:56 P.M.," which is the planetary hour before your birth time. Now move your finger across the page and stop under the column for Thursday; you will find the planet Jupiter. This means that this planet was ruling between 0:56 P.M. and 1:51 P.M., during which time you were born. Since Thursday is ruled by Jupiter and you were born during a Jupiter hour, blue is your Astral Color and your Soul Ray is expressed as "Jupiter/ Jupiter."

Let us suppose that you now meet someone born on Sunday, June 10, 1945, in New York City at 7:30 A.M. Turning to Table 6, "June and July, North Latitude," you again go to the column headed "35–45" and run your finger down to the time "8:18 A.M.," which is the first planetary hour after his or her birth time. You then move your finger upward to "7:04 A.M.," which is the planetary hour before his or her birth time. Now move your finger across the page to the column for Sunday; you will find the word *Merc*. This means that this planet was ruling between 7:04 A.M. and 8:18 A.M., during which time he or she was born. As Sunday is ruled by the Sun and his or her planetary hour is ruled by Mercury, the Soul Ray is expressed as "Sun/Mercury" and the colors are red/green.

What must be done now is to refer to the text following to see if these two Soul Rays are compatible. But let me try another example to make sure you truly understand this simple process. For instance, while most persons may know, or can find out, the time of their birth, the day of the week on which they were born has oftentimes been forgotten. To find the day of birth, use the perpetual calendar on pages 135–136.

Suppose you were born at 4:47 P.M. on June 12, 1949, in Detroit, Michigan. Detroit is located at 42°20′ north latitude.

CALENDARS—1800 TO 2050

DIRECTIONS FOR USE

Look for the year you want in the index at left. The number opposite each year is the number of the calendar to use for that year.

INDEX

1800...4	1828 10	1856 10	1884...10	1912 9	1940 9	1968 9	1996 9	2024 ..4	
1801...5	1829 .. 5	1857 .. 5	1885 .. 5	1913 .. 4	1941 4	1969 4	1997 4	2025 ..5	
1802...6	1830 6	1858 6	1886 6	1914 5	1942 5	1970 5	1998 5	2026 6	
1803...7	1831 7	1859 7	1887 7	1915 6	1943 6	1971 6	1999 6	2027 7	
1804...8	1832 8	1860 8	1888 8	1916 14	1944 14	1972 14	2000 .14	2028 14	
1805...2	1833 .. 3	1861 .. 3	1889 .. 3	1917 2	1945 2	1973 2	2001 2	2029 .. 2	
1806...3	1834 4	1862 4	1890 4	1918 3	1946 3	1974 3	2002 3	2030 .. 3	
1807...4	1835 5	1863 5	1891 5	1919 4	1947 4	1975 4	2003 4	2031 4	
1808.13	1836 13	1864 13	1892 13	1920 12	1948 12	1976 12	2004 12	2032 12	
1809...1	1837 1	1865 1	1893 1	1921 7	1949 7	1977 7	2005 7	2033 7	
1810...2	1838 .. 2	1866 .. 2	1894 2	1922 1	1950 1	1978 1	2006 1	2034 1	
1811...3	1839 3	1867 3	1895 3	1923 2	1951 2	1979 2	2007 2	2035 2	
1812.11	1840 11	1868 11	1896 11	1924 10	1952 10	1980 10	2008 10	2036 .10	
1813...6	1841 6	1869 6	1897 6	1925 5	1953 5	1981 5	2009 5	2037	
1814...7	1842 7	1870 7	1898 7	1926 6	1954 6	1982 6	2010 6	2038 7	
1815...1	1843 1	1871 1	1899 1	1927 7	1955 7	1983 7	2011 7	2039 7	
1816...9	1844 9	1872 9	1900 2	1928 8	1956 8	1984 8	2012 8	2040 8	
1817...4	1845 4	1873 4	1901 3	1929 3	1957 3	1985 3	2013 3	2041 .. 2	
1818...5	1846 5	1874 5	1902 4	1930 4	1958 4	1986 4	2014 4	2042 4	
1819...6	1847 6	1875 6	1903 5	1931 5	1959 5	1987 5	2015 5	2043 5	
1820.14	1848 14	1876 14	1904 13	1932 13	1960 13	1988 13	2016 13	2044 13	
1821...2	1849 2	1877 2	1905 1	1933 1	1961 1	1989 1	2017 1	2045 .. 1	
1822...3	1850 .. 3	1878 .. 3	1906 2	1934 2	1962 2	1990 2	2018 2	2046 .. 2	
1823...4	1851 4	1879 4	1907 3	1935 3	1963 3	1991 3	2019 3	2047 3	
1824.12	1852 12	1880 12	1908 11	1936 11	1964 11	1992 11	2020 11	2048 11	
1825...7	1853 .. 7	1881 .. 7	1909 6	1937 6	1965 6	1993 6	2021 6	2049 6	
1826...1	1854 .. 1	1882 .. 1	1910 7	1938 .. 7	1966 7	1994 7	2022 7	2050 7	
1827...2	1855...	1883 .. 2	1911 1	1939 .. 1	1967 1	1995 1	2023		

(Calendar grids numbered 1 through 6, each showing all twelve months: JANUARY, FEBRUARY, MARCH, APRIL, MAY, JUNE, JULY, AUGUST, SEPTEMBER, OCTOBER, NOVEMBER, DECEMBER with columns S M T W T F S)

10

JANUARY S M T W T F S
FEBRUARY S M T W T F S
MARCH S M T W T F S
APRIL S M T W T F S
MAY S M T W T F S
JUNE S M T W T F S
JULY S M T W T F S
AUGUST S M T W T F S
SEPTEMBER S M T W T F S
OCTOBER S M T W T F S
NOVEMBER S M T W T F S
DECEMBER S M T W T F S

14

JANUARY S M T W T F S
FEBRUARY S M T W T F S
MARCH S M T W T F S
APRIL S M T W T F S
MAY S M T W T F S
JUNE S M T W T F S
JULY S M T W T F S
AUGUST S M T W T F S
SEPTEMBER S M T W T F S
OCTOBER S M T W T F S
NOVEMBER S M T W T F S
DECEMBER S M T W T F S

9

JANUARY S M T W T F S
FEBRUARY S M T W T F S
MARCH S M T W T F S
APRIL S M T W T F S
MAY S M T W T F S
JUNE S M T W T F S
JULY S M T W T F S
AUGUST S M T W T F S
SEPTEMBER S M T W T F S
OCTOBER S M T W T F S
NOVEMBER S M T W T F S
DECEMBER S M T W T F S

13

JANUARY S M T W T F S
FEBRUARY S M T W T F S
MARCH S M T W T F S
APRIL S M T W T F S
MAY S M T W T F S
JUNE S M T W T F S
JULY S M T W T F S
AUGUST S M T W T F S
SEPTEMBER S M T W T F S
OCTOBER S M T W T F S
NOVEMBER S M T W T F S
DECEMBER S M T W T F S

8

JANUARY S M T W T F S
FEBRUARY S M T W T F S
MARCH S M T W T F S
APRIL S M T W T F S
MAY S M T W T F S
JUNE S M T W T F S
JULY S M T W T F S
AUGUST S M T W T F S
SEPTEMBER S M T W T F S
OCTOBER S M T W T F S
NOVEMBER S M T W T F S
DECEMBER S M T W T F S

12

JANUARY S M T W T F S
FEBRUARY S M T W T F S
MARCH S M T W T F S
APRIL S M T W T F S
MAY S M T W T F S
JUNE S M T W T F S
JULY S M T W T F S
AUGUST S M T W T F S
SEPTEMBER S M T W T F S
OCTOBER S M T W T F S
NOVEMBER S M T W T F S
DECEMBER S M T W T F S

7

JANUARY S M T W T F S
FEBRUARY S M T W T F S
MARCH S M T W T F S
APRIL S M T W T F S
MAY S M T W T F S
JUNE S M T W T F S
JULY S M T W T F S
AUGUST S M T W T F S
SEPTEMBER S M T W T F S
OCTOBER S M T W T F S
NOVEMBER S M T W T F S
DECEMBER S M T W T F S

11

JANUARY S M T W T F S
FEBRUARY S M T W T F S
MARCH S M T W T F S
APRIL S M T W T F S
MAY S M T W T F S
JUNE S M T W T F S
JULY S M T W T F S
AUGUST S M T W T F S
SEPTEMBER S M T W T F S
OCTOBER S M T W T F S
NOVEMBER S M T W T F S
DECEMBER S M T W T F S

Consulting the perpetual calendar, look for the year 1949 and find that you should use Calendar 7. Consulting Calendar 7 for June 12, you find that your day of birth was a Sunday.

You now consult Planetary Hour Table 6 for June and July in north latitude, and again look under the column headed "35–45" for the hour after your birth time. Running your finger down this column, you find the time "4:56 P.M.," which is the hour after. You then go up this column and find the hour "3:42 P.M.," which marks the planetary hour before your birth time. Moving your finger over the column under Sunday (your day of birth), you find the planet Mercury. This means that you were born during a Mercury hour on the day of the Sun. Hence, your Soul Ray is expressed as "Sun/Mercury" and your Astral Colors are red and green. Note that when we express our Soul Ray we always place the daily planetary ruler first (in this case the Sun) and the hourly planetary ruler second (Mercury).

Now suppose you meet someone born at 6:05 A.M. on November 29, 1940, in New York City. Again consulting the perpetual calendar, you look at the index for the year 1940 and find that the calendar for this year is 9. Consulting this calendar, you find that November 29 was a Friday. You now go to Planetary Hour Table 2, "November and February, North Latitude" to the column "35–45" as, once again, the latitude for New York City is 40°45′ north.

Now watch very carefully what happens here!

Looking at the sunrise hour given for this Friday, you find that sunrise took place at 6:56 A.M., which was after the 6:05 A.M. hour of birth. Hence, you must look to the hour before sunrise, which is the last planetary hour shown on the day previous. The time given for this is 5:46 A.M. In other words, although this person was born on Friday (ruled by Venus), in the planetary hour system the birth is governed by Jupiter (ruler of Thursday). Again, this is because all planetary hours are calculated from sunrise to sunrise.

Once more, moving your finger across the page in line with the 5:46 A.M., you now go to the column under Thursday and find the planet Sun. Hence, the Soul Ray for this person is Jupiter/Sun and the Astral Colors are blue and red.

SOUL RAY COMPATIBILITIES

Now that you know how to calculate your Soul Ray by using the various planetary hour charts, you must examine the meaning of the various Soul Ray combinations. Following is a chart of planetary correspondences:

Planet	Color	Day Ruled	Zodiac Sign	Element
Saturn	Violet	Saturday	Capricorn, Aquarius	Earth Air
Jupiter	Blue	Thursday	Sagittarius, Pisces	Fire Water
Mars	Yellow	Tuesday	Aries, Scorpio	Fire Water
Sun	Red	Sunday	Leo	Fire
Venus	Indigo	Friday	Taurus, Libra	Earth Air
Mercury	Green	Wednesday	Gemini, Virgo	Air Earth
Moon	Orange	Monday	Cancer	Water

Born on Sunday

Born on Sunday, you are under the rulership of the Sun and your Astral Color is red. You are highly creative and need to be at the center of attention most of the time. You envision yourself a person of authority even if you presently have none. You like to rule the roost and have things your own way. You do not like to be kept in the dark about anything going on around you. You want to know, and like the Kings of Old, often shoot the messenger when he brings bad news. Warm rooms and climates often appeal to you. You have a high idealistic sense combined with a flare for the dramatic. Any house you may visit will become *your* house and any party you attend is *yours* as well! You often come up with ideas much faster than you can do anything with. In fact, this is one of your drawbacks. You think and idealize, but often lack the follow-up to bring your ideals to fruition. As you are ruled by the Fire element, you will often consume those around you. Unless your friends and lovers want this, you may find yourself continually on the move.

In Love with Someone Born on Monday (Planet: Moon; Astral Color: Orange) You will find a strange sense of attraction, but not without difficulties. Monday Born will often want to stay at home while you want to go out. While you are somewhat set in your ways, he or she will always be in a state of change. Certainly your Fire will often boil Monday's Water! Or the reverse may be true and Monday's Water will extinguish your fiery passion for life in general. While you want to be out where the action is, Monday will want simply to stay at home. This is a difficult combination, but the attraction is here nonetheless.

In Love with Someone Born on Tuesday (Planetary Ruler: Mars; Astral Color: Yellow) You find a soul more in harmony with your inner flame. Here the fire of Aries blends with the fire of Leo. Be careful, however, because Mars also rules the fixed sign of Scorpio, whose watery depths can often make you boil. Certainly if you want an action-filled playmate, this is the right partner. You may clash over what it is you both should be doing, but do it you will without question. Somehow, in some way, you must be willing to let go of part of your authority and let Tuesday Born make a few of the decisions. If you can do this the relationship should go well. If you cannot, be prepared for the sparks to fly.

In Love with Someone Born on Wednesday (Planetary Ruler: Mercury; Astral Color: Green) We have yet another fine combination. Here the fire of the Sunday Born blends with the air of Gemini. Be on guard, however, that you do not let the Virgo

(Earth) side of the Wednesday Born put out your fire! While the Gemini side can be exciting and intriguing, the Virgo Ray can be limiting and unusually critical. When this happens, simply appeal to the Air element. Back down and breathe seven deep breaths! As is the case with many dual rulerships, a relationship that starts with a bang can deteriorate into a whimper. Whether or not this happens depends on no one but yourself.

In Love with Someone Born on Thursday (Planetary Ruler: Jupiter; Astral Color: Blue) Here again we find a Fire/Fire combination. The difficulty here is that both would want to make things happen. Sunday would want her parade, which, just coincidentally, is scheduled to take place when his band is off marching to a different drummer. You see, both Fire signs want to create in their own way. When this confrontation occurs, Thursday Born would withdraw, sulk, and revert to the hiding out offered by his or her Pisces side. When this happens, Sunday Born must be willing to back down—something which is not so easily done. Thursday Born also has a very deep religious side which when combined with an unusual amount of luck may be found grating by Sunday Born. Again, an attraction here but not without problems. It is simply that the life-style of each seems to come from different places.

In Love with Someone Born on Friday (Planetary Ruler: Venus; Astral Color: Indigo) We once again find a mixed bag. While the Libra side of the Friday Born would feed the flame of Sunday Born, the Taurus side might promise constriction. Here we find two beautiful people who can indeed fall deeply in love, but who have to be very careful that the ghosts of the past do not come out of the closets. It is indeed difficult to be a king or queen, and this is what Sunday Born is continually running into. What is needed is for the Sunday Born to become egoless—a task not without difficulty, indeed. Friday Born often just wants to be adored, cherished, and consumed. If Sunday Born can do just this without the moral trappings that often accompany one who "rules," this combination could work well indeed.

In Love with Someone Born on Saturday (Planetary Ruler: Saturn; Astral Color: Violet) We have perhaps the most impossible union of all. Unless the planetary hour of birth somehow overcomes the limitation set by the combination of the daily influence of Sun/Saturn, this combo promises disasterville all the way! It would be bad enough to surround the Fire of Sunday Born with the Earth of Saturday's child, but when we add the Air we have trouble afoot. Sunday Born would never seem able to please his or her Saturday mate. No matter what would be said or done, Sunday would feel put down if not put out!

In Love with Someone Also Born on Sunday We must look to the planetary hour of birth to determine compatibility. Simply put, there is always a danger when we mate with someone exactly the same as ourselves that we might become bored! Depending on the influence of the planetary hour, this combo can, or cannot, work!

Born on Monday

Born on Monday, you are under the rulership of the Moon, the Sign Cancer, which is of the Water element, and your Astral Color is orange. As the Moon is the most changeable of all the planets, here we find someone who is unusually changeable and appears to move quickly. There are deep feelings found here, though they are often hidden from others. When something is said or done to the Monday Born you can be sure that it will long be felt and remembered. Freedom is important here, but there is also a great need for the security of home, a good job, and a super love life. There will always be a continual struggle between security and the need to be free. How this will be reflected in one's love life is sometimes difficult to predict. If you are a woman born on this day, all the above qualities will be enhanced even moreso since the Moon is essentially feminine in its nature. If you are a man, you will possess a certain gentleness and easygoing nature women will find greatly attractive. Be careful, however, when dealing with the Monday Born, for what you see is not always what you get.

In Love with Someone Born on Tuesday (Planetary Ruler: Mars; Astral Color: Yellow) We find a Fire (Mars) and Water (Moon) combination. While there might be a great deal of attraction between Monday and Tuesday Born, since Mars also rules the Water Sign Scorpio, this attraction will soon vanish in the evening light! The heat of Mars would surely boil the water of the Moon, so much so that long periods apart from each other might be needed to save the relationship. Since Mars is masculine and the Moon feminine, there is great sexual energy, but without the Cosmic blessing to sustain it. If you are seeking only a one-night stand, this may be one of the best combinations you can find. If it's permanence you seek, however, stay away from this one!

In Love with Someone Born on Wednesday (Planetary Ruler: Mercury; Astral Color: Green) We find a somewhat neutral relationship, though possessing some possibility of working out on a very deep level. The potential for this combo working comes from the rulership of Virgo, an Earth Sign, by Mercury. Certainly the changeable nature of Mercury would match that of the Moon, but Water and Air contact each other only during a hurricane! Water and Earth, however, find a greater chance for stability, though too much Water (emotions) and we have mud! Once again, there is a need for caution, though with work this combo could sustain an OK relationship.

In Love with Someone Born on Thursday (Planetary Ruler: Jupiter; Astral Color: Blue) We find yet another Water/Fire combination. Although the nature of Jupiter and the Moon is certainly much softer than that of the Moon and Mars, we nonetheless have to take into consideration initial major differences of opinion. Of course, on a deeper level, as Jupiter rules the watery Pisces, this relationship could work, especially if both partners *own* their feelings. In other words, an enlightened couple could make this duo a happy one indeed. Monday Born would keep Thursday Born on his or her toes. Thursday Born would provide Monday Born with a feast of sensual delights. Certainly this combo would not be boring!

In Love with Someone Born on Friday (Planetary Ruler: Venus; Astral Color: Indigo) We have an excellent combination as the Water-born Moon's rays blend easily with the Venusian Earth. While there can be occasional disagreements owing to the sub-rulership of Friday Born's Venus over Air-bound Libra, this is for all intents and purposes a fine union. One danger here, however, is that the relationship may become too feminine, or too *Yin* as the Chinese would say. There might not be enough get up and go to make this union accomplish what the parties mutually desire. This would certainly be a combo that is laid back in all areas of life.

In Love with Someone Born on Saturday (Planetary Ruler: Saturn; Astral Color: Violet) We find a workable combination in which one of the partners might be considerably older (or certainly at least wiser!). Here, once again, we have Water and Earth, or more precisely, Water and Earth/Air. If Monday Born will allow Saturday Born to rule the roost, this duo could be quite successful. Surely, Saturday Born will find the light of the Moon desirable for dancing in, while the Moonchild will find Saturday's stable shoulder a good one to learn on. Occasional spats? Of course. But over the long haul, this is a rather workable and rewarding union.

In Love with Someone Born on Sunday See Sunday Born.

In Love with Someone Also Born on Monday We must look to the planetary hour to determine if there's harmony here.

Born on Tuesday

Born on Tuesday, with your planetary ruler Mars and your Astral Color yellow, you are under the influence of fiery (and watery) Mars. A difficult combination? You bet! The power of Aries and having to be right and first above all else comes to the fore here. This is certainly the day on which someone who "does" is born, rather than someone who is "done to." In fact, this is somewhat of a problem for the Tuesday Born. One must be in control and have things his or her own way. If you are a woman born on this day, or in love with such a creature, expect to find an abundance of masculine, or *Yang*, energy. The Tuesday Born always wears the pants—even if they belong to him!

In Love with Someone Born on Wednesday (Planetary Ruler: Mercury; Astral Color: Green) We have a very exciting, sensual duality. The Fire of Mars consumes the Air of Mercury. As long as Mercury does not object to being eaten alive, this is a combo that promises a sex life made in paradise, for even the subrulerships of Earth and Water, Virgo and Scorpio are in divine order and harmony. Certainly one born on Tuesday could not do better than to unite with one born on Wednesday. Expect sparks to fly from this one and a fire that could last a lifetime!

In Love with Someone Born on Thursday (Planetary Ruler: Jupiter; Astral Color: Blue) We have a combination of two Fire Signs that *should* get along, but might find some unexpected clashes. You see everything that exists in the astrological or spiritual planes is mirrored in the physical world. Since one of the ways to extinguish a forest fire is to build a backfire so there is no fuel, thereby using fire to extinguish fire, the combination of two Fire Signs can work likewise. Both are likely to want to call the shots at the same time and in the same way. If one perseveres, however, this could be a good combination, though expect emotions to run deep since both subrulers are of the watery element. Thursday Born will no doubt interject the ethical or philosophical reasons why something should be done or not done, while Tuesday Born will always look at the practical point of view. If you like working hard at a relationship, give this one a try!

In Love with Someone Born on Friday (Planetary Ruler: Venus; Astral Color: Indigo) Expect a great deal of attraction but lacking in duration. Certainly when Mars and Venus come together sparks fly. Whether this combo can work depends on whether Friday Born is willing to play second fiddle to Tuesday Born. Remember that Fire can rest on earth, but Earth placed on fire extinguishes it! In this case, Tuesday must be willing to let go of always doing things his or her own way. If Friday insists on calling the shots, this relationship is doomed from the start. This is the kind of union, however, in which one can't live *with* or *without* the other person. So in the words of wise ol' Zolar, be sure you use the potholder when you handle this kettle! 'Nuff said!

In Love with Someone Born on Saturday (Planetary Ruler: Saturn; Astral Color: Violet) Once again we have the awfully trying Fire/Earth combination. Even if both partners try extra hard and revert to the subrulers, Air and Water, there is still not a great deal of harmony here. In fact, Saturn/Mars combos often cause a great deal of anger, so this could very well be a relationship in which you'd expect to find tears and frustration. Why is it we always desire to go where we intuitively know we shouldn't? This is a mystery even Zolar hasn't figured out. One thing is sure, and that is that there is always an attraction between Fire and Earth. Tuesday Born wants the stability of Saturday Born and Saturday Born wants the excitement he or she thinks that Tuesday offers. Be careful; ginger in the neighbor's garden always smells more pungent.

In Love with Someone Born on Sunday See Sunday Born.

In Love with Someone Born on Monday See Monday Born.

In Love with Someone Also Born on Tuesday Look to the planetary hour to determine compatibility.

Born on Wednesday

Born on Wednesday, with your planetary ruler Mercury and your Astral Color Green, you are under the rulership of Mercury, an Air/Earth element. Here we find scintillating wit and excitement that always accompany the true dilettante! It will be very difficult for you to get a fix on the Wednesday Born. Here today and gone tomorrow may apply to every avenue of life—even you! Remember that Gemini is the Sign of Twins, so you are dealing here not with one person but with two. Whatever agreements you think are reached may have indeed to be renegotiated with partner B. This can be exciting and even fun—if you don't weaken. On the other hand, the subruler Virgo (Earth) will always suggest that stability (like prosperity) is just around the corner. But that's where it may always be . . . and the block is a large one!

In Love with Someone Born on Thursday (Planetary Ruler: Jupiter; Astral Color: Blue) Here we find a most complex relationship. As Wednesday born resonates as BOTH air (Gemini) and earth (Virgo), while Thursday born is fire (Sagittarius) AND water (Pisces), the possibility for both an unusually intense and stormy relationship abound here. If an actor in this play, expect (and learn to live with) the unexpected!

In Love with Someone Born on Friday (Planetary Ruler: Mars; Astral Color: Yellow) We find a truly head/heart duo. Mercury, Wednesday's ruler, rules the mind and Venus, Friday's ruler, the emotions. Do you think you'll have trouble here? You bet you will! Head and heart struggles are always the most difficult to extricate ourselves from, especially when they exist deep within our own nature. This is a most difficult combination, somewhat like flypaper—awfully attractive to the fly but a heck of a mess once you land on it! Notice, too, that the subrulers, Virgo (Mercury) and Libra (Venus) are also of the Air/Earth vibration. Sure, Air and Earth meet. But what happens when they do? A duststorm? I'd suggest staying away from this one.

In Love with Someone Born on Saturday (Planetary Ruler: Saturn; Astral Color: Violet) We have yet another Air/Earth combination. While the flighty Wednesday Born Mercury is attracted to the solidarity of Saturday Born Saturn, this is not an easy duo to say the least. Like the Wednesday/Friday duo, Earth and Air just don't cut the mustard, as Granny used to say. While one of the partners may be older, wealthier, or more established, this is certainly not a union made in heaven. Saturday would put the brakes on Wednesday, causing a great deal of inner (and outer) tension. A graphic example of this particular union would be driving the car without first releasing the hand brake. Sooner or later, something has to give. Stay away from this combination—if you can.

In Love with Someone Born on Sunday See Sunday Born.

In Love with Someone Born on Monday See Monday Born.

In Love with Someone Born on Tuesday See Tuesday Born.

In Love with Someone Also Born on Wednesday Look to the planetary hour to determine compatibility.

Born on Thursday

Born on Thursday, with your planetary ruler Jupiter and your Astral Color blue, you are under the rulership of Jupiter and the Signs Sagittarius and Pisces. You couldn't find a more generous person than those born on this day. Optimism for the now and the future prevails throughout all aspects of the Thursday Born. Being a Fire Sign, there is a great deal of creative energy that can be shot out, just like arrows, in all different directions. If you want someone who will make you feel like a real woman or a real man, pick this person as your mate. Remember, however, that the Pisces side of this Ray has deep emotions, even though they are not usually shown or sometimes shared. Add to this a great love of travel and you have a gem indeed. But always remember, Thursday Borns need long leashes, for above all else they worship freedom!

In Love with Someone Born on Friday (Planetary Ruler: Venus; Astral Color: Indigo) Here you will find a genuine god or goddess. Remember, however, the lessons of Greek mythology, which taught us that such celestial beings are often to be worshiped but seldom to be touched. In short, while there is a warm, close feeling about this combo, in the long run it will most likely not work. Why? Once again, we have a Fire and Earth sandwich that, while pleasing to the taste, often brings indigestion. Once more, it all depends on who's on top. If Fire, OK. If Earth, not. Even on the deeper side, Thursday Born Pisces and Friday Born Librans don't seem to make it much easier. If you are looking for a playmate, this might work. If you're looking for Twin Soul, look very carefully before you leap!

In Love with Someone Born on Saturday (Planetary Ruler: Saturn; Astral Color: Violet) We find a push-pull relationship seldom equaled. Here, Thursday Born wants to expand, which is its Jupiter nature, while Saturn wants to contract, its natural essence. Again there is certainly an attraction, but one might find this duo only if a true glutton for punishment! Do you really enjoy fighting, kissing, and making up? Might it not be easier to switch rather than fight? These are all factors that both parties of this match *must* take into consideration.

In Love with Someone Born on Sunday See Sunday Born.

In Love with Someone Born on Monday See Monday Born.

In Love with Someone Born on Tuesday See Tuesday Born.

In Love with Someone Born on Wednesday See Wednesday Born.

In Love with Someone Also Born on Thursday Look to the planetary hour to determine compatibility.

Born on Friday

Born on a Friday, with your planetary ruler Venus and your Astral Color Indigo, you are under the rulership of the planet Venus and the Signs Taurus (Earth) and Libra (Air). Here, we find a person with great idealism blended with a high degree of practicality. Venus being the goddess of love, we have here someone who *must* be in a relationship in order to be happy. There are no ifs, ands, or buts about it. Being a feminine planet, expect to find a gentle and highly sensual soul who usually knows what he or she wants—and usually gets it. This is the day on which true romantics are often born. They will court and woo you until you find yourself lost in their arms. If other signs portend, you can't go too far wrong by loving the Friday Born.

In Love with Someone Born on Saturday (Planetary Ruler: Saturn; Astral Color: Violet) We have an excellent combination, though on the surface it would appear highly unlikely that Venus and Saturn could successfully unite. Saturday Born suggests the ultimate in material practicality while Friday Born postures the highest idealism coupled with deep emotions. In other words, here we have a rather mundane but highly successful match in the heavens, so to speak. Both ruling planets have as their primary element Earth, Venusian Taurus and Saturnian Capricorn. Likewise, both planets have Air Signs as their subruler, Libra and Aquarius. It is almost as if the rarefied air of the Capricorn goatfish actually "needs" the soft gentleness of the Libran. Also, from yet another viewpoint, as the Saturday Born is usually quite materially successful, such would easily provide a comfortable base from which the Friday Born can enjoy his or her dreams without concern for such little things as paying the rent!

In Love with Someone Born on Sunday See Sunday Born.

In Love with Someone Born on Monday See Monday Born.

In Love with Someone Born on Tuesday See Tuesday Born.

In Love with Someone Born on Wednesday See Wednesday Born.

In Love with Someone Born on Thursday See Thursday Born.

In Love with Someone Also Born on Friday Look to the planetary hour to determine compatibility.

Born on Saturday

Born on Saturday, with your planetary ruler Saturn and your Astral Color Violet, you are under the primary rulership of Saturn and the Earth Sign Capricorn. Here we have the earmark of someone who knows what he or she wants in every area of life, who goes after it, and who gets it. While there is a certain rigidity to this earthbound actor or actress, mentally we have a person who is capable of great depths of thought and concentration. Because of this single purpose of mind, the secret of the true magician, these folks possess the power to visualize into being anything they so desire. I do not wish to suggest that you have a highly enlightened mystic or seer here, however. On the contrary, you have someone who simply does what comes naturally. Success in life or in relationships is as commonplace as drinking the morning cup of coffee. You are someone strong and quite predictable.

In Love with Someone Born on Sunday See Sunday Born.

In Love with Someone Born on Monday See Monday Born.

In Love with Someone Born on Tuesday See Tuesday Born.

In Love with Someone Born on Wednesday See Wednesday Born.

In Love with Someone Born on Thursday See Thursday Born.

In Love with Someone Born on Friday See Friday Born.

In Love with Someone Also Born on Saturday Look to the planetary hour to determine compatibility.

UNDER THE MICROSCOPE

Now that I have explained the primary Soul Ray as determined by the day on which you were born, some mention must be made of the use of the primary hour of birth.

As you will recall in the previous examples, each person's Soul

Ray is expressed in terms of the planet ruling the day and the hour on which he or she was born. Hence each Soul Ray is expressed as a "two planet" figure, with the first planet meaning the day and the second meaning the hour—Saturn/Jupiter, Mars/Venus, and so on. Needless to say, it is of great importance to take the hour of birth into consideration. While the Ray of the day of birth of both parties may be in harmony, the Ray of the hour of birth may suggest conflicts.

To determine whether or not the hour of birth is in harmony, simply refer to what I said concerning the compatibility of the various days. For instance, in the example just given, if you refer to the paragraph under Born on Tuesday, entitled In Love with Someone Born on Saturday, you will find that this combination is a difficult one (see page 145). To compare the planetary hour of birth, go to the section entitled Born on Thursday and refer to the paragraph entitled In Love with Someone Born on Friday (see page 147). Here, once again you find portents of a somewhat difficult union. Hence, it would seem highly unlikely that these particular Soul Rays would find happiness.

See how easy it is? Remember, too, that you can use this method to figure out your relationships with your boss, your mother, your father, or even your children. Why this very simple ancient technique hasn't gained more popularity is unknown. But one thing is sure, and you can count on Zolar for that. It works!

10

Using Planetary Hours to Make Decisions

★
★
★ ★
★ ★
★ ★

Fortune at some hour to all is kind;
The lucky have whole days which still they choose;
The unlucky have but hours and those they lose.

—CHARLES DRYDEN

Now that you have mastered the use of planetary hours and color to predict the outcome of every relationship, you can extend your knowledge by using the mysteries of time and space to help guide you in your daily activities. To do this you have simply to pay attention to the time on the clock when various events happen. For those who are astrologers, this practice is already well known and is the basis for what is called Horary Astrology, or the Astrology of the Hour. A Horary Astrologer simply casts a horoscope for the time at which he or she is asked a particular question by a client. It is believed that such a horoscope chart always contains the answer to whatever question has been raised.

This idea finds its origin in the teachings of Aristotle, who taught that all knowledge was recollection. Hence, one cannot *ask* a question without already knowing the answer, which, in this case, appears in the horoscope cast by the astrologer. The unconscious mind of the client causes a particular question to be asked *only at the time* when an answer is already in existence. Should the mind of the client be unclear as to the framing of the question, however, such lack of clarity will be reflected in the chart cast by the astrologer, thereby rendering the question unanswerable. In this case, the astrologer will advise the client to rethink his or her question and call again at another time. Later, if the mind of the inquirer is clear, an answer will appear in the new chart. If not, the inquirer will again be advised to rethink his or her question and then telephone again. Seldom, however, are more than one or two calls required before an answer is shown in the chart.

When it comes to questions concerning the outcome of certain future events, such are also answerable by this process. In some strange way, then, *future* events are predictable by *present* time! Before the advent of the ability to calculate the positions of the various planets before they actually occurred, all astrological predictions used this system, as all that was known of the movement of the planets was based on past or present observations. While casting horoscopes usually requires certain technical knowledge, or access to a computer, our new knowledge of the mysterious color connection simplifies this process and makes it easily usable by all.

You see, there is a definite connection between a particular planetary hour, its color connection, and events that occur at a particular time and place. This means that if we can understand this connection, we can easily use this information to gain insight as to what is likely to happen to us in the future, simply by observing the time at which various interactions with other persons happen.

Mystics throughout the ages and some psychologists such as Carl G. Jung have suggested that there are truly no accidents in the universe. Thus, *when* an event happens is as important as the actual event itself. Before the advent of so-called scientific testing by physicians, following the injunction of Hippocrates that "a physician who does not have knowledge of astrology should not call himself a physician," horoscope charts were routinely cast for the moment a person took ill. Called *decumbiture* charts, such were believed to indicate both the cause of the illness and whether or not the patient would recover.

Having personal experience of such charts, I can say without hesitation that they are amazingly accurate and often hold secrets unavailable by other means. But alas, in their search for scientific truth, most physicians have forgotten the words of their patron saint—as well as his injunction that the physician should first and foremost do no harm. One physician, however—L. D. Broughton of New York—in fact published an excellent textbook in 1898 entitled *The Elements of Astrology,* in which he discussed at great length the use of planetary hours. Although this book is long out of print and virtually impossible to find today, these comments by Dr. Broughton are certainly worthy of our notice, and clearly set the scene for what we can glean from the use of this simple but extraordinary process:

> The signification of the Planetary Hours is very ancient and was approved and used by the Arabians and nearly all of the Eastern and Asiatic nations; and the hours are so made use of even to the present day. They are confirmed by astrologers generally, and are of great use in all ordinary business, though they are not of that efficacy or influence as the calculations of the movements of the heavenly bodies, for the finding out and choosing a special time to commence any new business or important undertaking, and which time does also sympathize or agree with the horoscope of the native.
>
> By observing the Tables of Planetary Hours, the reader, even if he knows nothing of astrology, may choose fortunate periods to begin any particular undertaking, or removal, or to commence any important change in his life.
>
> I have made thousands of observations and calculated the positions of the planets for the time people have married, or made any particular change of their life, such as removal,

or going into any new business, etc., and it almost invariably proved the truth of astrology; for when they have made these changes at unfortunate periods or under what are termed evil aspects, they almost invariably ended unfortunately, or some way disastrously to the parties. But when they made important changes, or commenced new undertakings under fortunate aspects, they generally turned out successfully to the persons who commenced them.

To use the planetary hours in this way, then, we have to pay particular attention to a number of factors. First, we must note on the clock, or our watch, exactly what time (day or night) we receive a particular communication or are greeted by a particular person. By *time,* we mean the Standard Time of the particular time zone in which we live—Eastern, Central, Mountain, or Pacific Time. In other words, this is the time that appears on your clock, with the exception of Daylight Savings Time, during which an hour must be deducted. While planetary hours were created by the gods, Daylight Savings Time was created by humans.

Once you have noted the time at which you receive a particular communication, you must then consult the Planetary Hour Tables (see pages 128–133) to determine which planets and what color influence is at work. This will tell us a great deal about the magical forces behind this communication.

Second, you will also wish to note the nature of the communication. What has been said? What has been talked about? What has been offered? This is done to see if the planet ruling the nature of the communication is in harmony with the hour at which it has been presented.

For instance, suppose you have been offered a chance to make a sales presentation to a company with whom you are not currently doing business. At the time you receive this inquiry you note that Saturn was ruling the hour. As you will shortly learn, the Sun rules honor and promotions. However, since Saturn, the planet of delays and obstruction, rules at this time, it is highly unlikely that this presentation will ever take place. Knowing this in advance could save you countless hours of preparation for a meeting that is not ever likely to take place. So, you must begin to pay particular attention to both the messenger as well as the message.

Still another use of the planetary hours is to also inquire as to the Birth date (and planetary ruler) of the person who brings you a particular communication. For instance, suppose your messenger was born under the Sun Sign Aries (March 21 to April 20). The ruling planet of Aries is Mars, which is considered a negative planet except in those matters connected with martial activities—athletics, military, iron, steel, all affairs requiring great physical effort. For such a person to suggest this proposal, especially under the same Saturn hour, would surely suggest a probable negative outcome.

Now suppose you did not know the birthday of your messenger, but noted the colors he or she was wearing. Would this not also tell you something of the real nature of this proposal? Most certainly! For example, should the messenger be a Leo (born July 23 to August 22) wearing red, and should he approach you during an hour ruled by the Sun, you can rest assured that the proposal will result in great success!

To help you judge the varying planetary and color influences, the following chart may prove helpful.

Astrological Sign	Rulership Dates	Ruling Planet	Color
Aries	Mar. 21–April 20	Mars	Yellow
Taurus	April 21–May 20	Venus	Indigo
Gemini	May 21–June 21	Mercury	Green
Cancer	June 22–July 22	Moon	Orange
Leo	July 23–Aug. 22	Sun	Red
Virgo	Aug. 23–Sept. 22	Mercury	Green
Libra	Sept. 23–Oct. 22	Venus	Indigo
Scorpio	Oct. 23–Nov. 21	Mars	Yellow
Sagittarius	Nov. 22–Dec. 21	Jupiter	Blue
Capricorn	Dec. 22–Jan. 19	Saturn	Violet
Aquarius	Jan. 20–Feb. 18	Saturn	Violet
Pisces	Feb. 19–March 20	Jupiter	Blue

Since every hour is ruled by a particular color and planet, it is decidedly good for some activities and bad for others. The words *good* and *bad* as used here have nothing to do with moral judgments, however; rather, they refer to the nature of the Cosmic vibrations at work at a particular moment in time and space.

To make even clearer exactly what use one might make of the planetary hours, Dr. Broughton offered the following general guidelines.

Sun hours (red) are especially good for anyone seeking favors or promotions from persons in authority, such as an employer or parent. This is not a good time for commencing the construction of anything or buying new clothing. It is also not a good time to move into a new office or new house. One should also not spend money, or pay it out in any way, during this hour. It is also not a good time during which to become ill, as such would suggest a serious illness.

Venus hours (indigo) are good for seeking favors from women, especially if one is a man. It is also a good time to start a short business or pleasure trip, but not a long one. It is a good time to relax or play any sports. It is a good time to take any drugs, remedies, or vitamins. If someone becomes ill during this hour, Broughton suggests that the illness is probably due to overindulgence—too much rich food or drink, or not enough sleep the night before. This is also a good time to commence any business that relates to women. It's also a good time to propose marriage. This is a good time for both men and women to interact with other women.

Mercury hours (green) center on communications. Buying, selling, writing letters, sending faxes, lending or borrowing money are just a few of the activities that come to the fore at this time. This is not a good time for contracting marriages, however, or buying real estate, or to return to one's home after a long trip. It is also not a good time to hire an employee. One can seek favors from wealthy or prominent persons during this hour, but a Sun hour may be even more advantageous.

Moon hours (orange) are a good time for a man to seek favors from women, a good time to purchase pets, and a good time to take or send one's children to school. It is also a good time to begin a lawsuit and also for foreign travel. However, when one returns home, one should do so under a Venus hour.

Saturn hours (violet) are bad times to commence long trips and portend small success for any ventures started, or first proposed at this time. It is also not a good time to take any medication or vitamin supplements, or medical treatment unless an emergency. It is not a good time to hire employees, as it is said they will most likely be lazy and not work out. It is also not a good time to don new clothing or to have any kind of cosmetic improvement, hair-cuts, or hair or skin treatments. It is an excellent time for real-estate transactions, however. It is also a good time for commencing any farming activities, planting a garden, plowing. It is not a good time to borrow or lend money. Lastly, should one become ill during this hour, the illness should be considered serious and proper medical attention sought.

Jupiter hours (blue) are especially good for dealing with persons in authority, civil service, lawyers, judges, or senators to obtain favors. It is a good time to leave one's house or office and to commence business trips that will end successfully. It is a good time for planting and also for lending or borrowing money. It is also a good time to enter into contracts. Should one become ill during this hour, he or she will recover very quickly.

Mars hours (yellow) are not a time to commence anything of importance, as overenthusiasm will be dominant. This is a time during which passion rather than reason is the ruling force. Only if one is involved with Martial activities—military, police, athletics—should this hour be considered positive. It is also not a good hour for any surgical procedures, unless absolutely necessary. It is a decidedly bad time to commence any business or personal trips.

Now, to give you further insight into how to use planetary hours, following is a list of key words for the various hours, which will enable you to start evaluating the usefulness of this practice.

Sun (red) key words: King, ruler, president of any company, chief executive, manager, department head, one's father (or father-surrogate), promotion, gold, shows, expositions, honors, recognitions, royal treatment, great success, judges, the boss, honors, grants, glory, fame, achievement, amusement parks, dignitaries, employment, foreman, halls, important people, palaces, political elections, sporting events, theaters.

Venus (indigo) key words: Money, art, possessions, fun, harmony, partnerships, florists, jewelry, entertainers, designers, agreements, treaties, artists, theaters, laziness, young girls and women, love matters, women's clothing, love affairs, dancers, personal property, society people, diplomats, architects, adolescence, musical instruments.

Mercury (green) key words: Communications, letters, documents, messengers, reports, transportation, commerce, young people (in general), students and teachers, accountants and bookkeeepers, secretaries, merchants, newspapers and journalists, postal workers, schemes and tricksters, railroads, sales promotion, brothers and sisters, speakers, the press, tourists, travel agents, short trips, writers, written documents, working class (in general), waitresses, typists, visitors, relatives (in general), deliveries, dogs, fellow employees, telephone calls, mail, printers, health foods, editors.

Moon (orange) key words: Women (in general), female qualities such as intuition, receptivity, nurturing; sailors, common people, female occupations, women officials, sailors and water occupations; household and domestic affairs, the electorate, one's mother (along with Venus), subjects of popular interest, ambassadors, antiques, planting, beverages, babies, change (in general), chefs, alcoholics.

Saturn (violet) key words: Frustration, containment, limitations, boundaries, Father Time, reality check, old persons, one's father, corporations and corporate personnel, landlords, real estate, wise counselors, civil servants, conservative people and businesses, anything or anyone that restricts, age, monks, stockholders, administrators.

Jupiter (blue) key words: Abundance, great luck, religion, gamblers, speculation, church, long-distance travel, publishers and publishing, universities and schools of learning, doctors, judges, lawyers, capitalists, sports, success, generosity, clergy, zoos, gambling, ashrams, adult education.

Mars (yellow) key words: Boldness, aggression, war, fire, young men, athletes, soldiers, police, butchers, dentists, athletic contests, barbers, violence, risk taking, pioneers, researchers, surgeons, abortions, carpenters, accidents, burns, enthusiasm, mathematics ability, guns, engineers, guards, quarrels, steel.

Although this list is somewhat lengthy, getting familiar with it will certainly enable you to begin to think about, and notice, the connection between the time on the clock when an event occurs and its hidden meaning.

At first you may find it hard to accept that such a mysterious connection really exists between *you* and absolutely everything that happens in your life. But I assure you that if you begin to pay attention, and apply this technique on a daily basis, you will attain a new level of awareness. But just to make absolutely certain that you fully understand how to use this process, let us consider an example.

Again, the first thing you must do is determine your location by latitude. This information can be obtained by consulting any map. Suppose you are living in Boston, Massachusetts, which is located at 42° north latitude. By consulting the tables beginning on page 128, you will see a listing for latitudes 35–45 degrees north. Now consider the month you are currently in and turn to the particular table for which it applies. Once found, look for today's day and note it as well. Assuming you live in Boston and the month is November, you turn to Table 2 (page 129). Suppose today is Thursday and the time on the clock is 10:30 A.M. Run your finger down the "35–45" column, and stop at the line indicating 10:18 A.M., which is the start of this particular planetary hour. Now move your finger to the left until you come to the column "TH" (Thursday), at which you find the word *Merc*, indicating that this planet (Mercury) and its corresponding color, green, rule at this time. By consulting the words given earlier, you know exactly which activities are favored at this time and those which are not.

Suppose this was the time, many weeks ago, when you had scheduled an interview with a prospective employee. All other indications being favorable, as Mercury rules employment, you would certainly now be justified in hiring this employee based on your new insight!

Let's take another example. We live in Atlanta, Georgia, whose latitude is 33 degrees north. It is April, the day is Monday, and the time is 4 P.M. Turning to Table 4 (page 131), we once again look to the column marked "25–35" and run our finger down this column to come to "3:09 P.M.," the time before our 4:00 P.M. clock time. We now run our finger across the page to the column for Monday, where we find Jupiter (color blue) indicated. In this case, some contracts have just come to us from our attorney for signature. As Jupiter clearly rules such things as lawyers and contracts, signing at this time portends a successful outcome in this matter.

In other words, the correct use of planetary hours enables us to determine exactly what we should do at a particular time and place, in order to carry out the intent of the Cosmic.

While it is often said that it is not my will but Thy Will that should be followed, very rarely are we told how this will is to be ascertained. By the use of planetary hours and the magick of color, however, the difficulty is easily resolved.

If, dear reader, you are still doubtful as to exactly how planetary hours can work, may I suggest that you give them a try for a few days or for a week or for a month. I am certain that, if you do as I did, you will be convinced of their efficacy.

In conclusion, the following by the astrologer Llewellyn George, in his long out-of-print work *The Sky Is the Limit,* best explains why planetary hours are important:

> We are human generators. Each being projects about himself
> an influence which is received and felt by others consciously

or unconsciously, and the quality of this influence largely determines the attitude of others towards us. Some individuals emit an electric atmosphere, some a magnetic, and some electro-magnetic. To illustrate: Electric natures are repellent. They object to thoughts, ideas and customs unless they appeal to their inner natures, but they quicken, enliven and inspire others. The magnetic natures attract and assimilate thoughts and ideas and invite assistance or cooperation. The electromagnetic nature is volatile and adaptable; at times attractive and at other times repellent. Such persons respond quickly to passing vibrations and are ever ready for something new.

Llewellyn goes on to suggest that it takes only a "little practice and observation" for anyone to determine which planetary hours are "most important." He suggests that we begin to note which planets are ruling when we receive good news, when we accomplish something special, or when we feel especially good. "As consciousness of life develops, that is, as we unfold and refine ourselves, the more correctly do we respond to celestial influence," he adds.

"The heavens [planetary and starry system] declare the glory [wisdom] of God, and the firmament sheweth His handiwork. Day unto day uttereth speech, and night unto night sheweth knowledge," says the Nineteenth Psalm. Llewellyn George concludes, "We are all receptive to this 'glory,' but in different degrees. The nature of our response depends upon the state of our understanding, and the effects or results of our actions are determined in accordance with the degree of our knowledge of Natural Law. Few, indeed, are they who have attained the full measure of their horoscopal indications and possibilities."

11

The Color Magick of Gemstones

Pearls and other jewels as well as metals and plants, applied directly to the human skin, exercise an electro-magnetic influence over the physical cells. Man's body contains carbon and various metallic elements that are present also in plants, metals and jewels. The discoveries of the rishis in these fields will doubtless receive confirmation someday from physiologists. Man's sensitive body, with its electrical life currents, is a center of many mysteries as yet unexplored.

—PARAMAHANSA YOGANANDA, *Autobiography of a Yogi*

While the idea that various stones and gems contain magical properties is of great antiquity, the correct use of such stones is seldom written about or taught. Almost everyone knows his or her astrological birthstone, but the esoteric traditions that accompany this connection have, unfortunately, been lost through the passage of time. I say *unfortunately* because, as a result of misunderstandings, many persons wear gemstones that can actually cause ill health or bad luck. These ill-chosen gems can affect the very delicate vibrations surrounding the physical body that compose what has been called the "human aura."

But let me take you back in time to when I first became aware of the way in which gemstones work. I had just received a call from a young woman, a tennis pro, who wished a homeopathic consultation with me in my New York office. Her complaint was the sudden onset of arthritis in both hands. After conducting my routine analysis, which included a discussion of her diet and life-style, I was somewhat puzzled as to why symptoms of arthritis should appear so suddenly. I then noticed that she was wearing an unusual amount of rings and bracelets on both hands and wrists. When I inquired as to when she first started wearing this jewelry, she responded that she had purchased it all about six months previous, while on a vacation in the U.S. Southwest.

"Was this before the arthritis appeared?" I asked.

"Well, I never thought about it before, but it was!" she replied.

Suddenly, I had the answer. I told her to remove all her rings and bracelets, as I wished to check each one with my pendulum through radiesthesia by matching them with her witness, a saliva specimen. In each case, the pendulum indicated that her electro-magnetic fields conflicted with the energy given off by the tur-quoise and silver jewelry she had been wearing! I suggested that she not ever wear it again.

"But I love silver and turquoise," she protested. "You know it's made by the Indians."

"Well, then let the Indians wear it," I said, "because it's not good for you!"

After a few additional arguments, she agreed to give up wearing the jewelry for a few weeks on a trial basis. Some time later, I received a call from her to say that I had been right, and that all the arthritis symptoms had magically disappeared. This instance was in turn followed by others, somewhat similar, in which the wrong use of gemstones proved detrimental to the health of those who wore them.

At first, I reasoned wrongly that the influence of the jewelry on the person wearing it was due to a relationship with the person who had originally given it. For instance, a woman continued to wear a ring given to her by her ex-husband! Of course, she didn't "feel" right when she wore his ring. How could she when she didn't feel right about him? This made perfectly sound, psychological sense. But I came to learn that while this might be true psychologically, it was decidedly bad metaphysics.

One day, while perusing Paramahansa Yogananda's *Autobiography of a Yogi*, I recalled the chapter in which he describes being told by his Master to wear an astrological bangle in order to counter some upcoming negative planetary influences that would affect his health, and especially his liver. Surely, if wearing a particular gemstone could work in this way, then wearing the right stone must have some preventive value as well!

It then occurred to me that for gemstones to truly work in this magical way, there must be some connection between them and one's horoscope and aura, the latter being the name we give to the various electromagnetic fields that surround us. So off I went in search of an answer, which was to be found in the writings of an Indian physician, Dr. A. K. Bhattacharyya. According to Bhattacharyya and other Indian mystics, the energy given off by each gemstone resonates with various colors, vitamins, minerals, endocrine glands, and a particular planet in one's horoscope chart. Every gemstone is in essence a miniature color projector that, if properly selected and worn, can alter the health of that person in much the same way an acupuncture treatment works to raise one's immune system.

Just as there are various pulses, which when interpreted by a skilled acupuncturist will lead him or her to choose various points for treatment, so does one's horoscope contain similar codings. Unlike acupuncture, however, should a person wear an incorrect gemstone, he or she can actually short-circuit the magnetic fields, thereby resulting in ill health or bad luck.

While many people have chosen to wear a gemstone based on their astrological sign—a topaz for Sagittarians, for example—if that stone is not in harmony with the person's horoscope chart (which must be accurately calculated for the time, place, and date of birth), the practice will not be successful.

No doubt this original teaching of the ancients, through the passage of time, became watered down to the oversimplified assignment of only one gemstone for each Sign of the Zodiac. On the next page is a chart that will serve to illustrate this very important connection. Study it well.

How do we use this system? First, one must have an accurately calculated horoscope chart that contains an aspectarian showing the interactions of the various planets. (See Appendix B.) In other words, we need to know how every planet is aspected. This is simply another way of saying how many degrees of longitude each planet is from another.

For those who are not familiar with such things, the major aspects are as follows:

Conjunction: Two or more planets are 6 to 8 degrees apart in the same Sign of the Zodiac, or adjacent Signs. Considered positive or negative, depending on the planets involved.

Sextile: Two or more planets are 60 degrees apart, plus or minus 6 to 8 degrees. Considered positive.

Square: Two or more planets are 90 degrees apart, plus or minus 6 to 8 degrees. Considered negative.

Trine: Two or more planets are 120 degrees apart, plus or minus 6 to 8 degrees. Considered positive.

Opposition: Two or more planets are 180 degrees apart, plus or minus 6 to 8 degrees. Considered negative.

Second, we must examine the aspects of each planet to determine whether it is positively or negatively aspected. For instance, suppose the Sun in your horoscope is in conjunction with the planet Jupiter. This is considered a positive aspect, as Jupiter is the planet of expansion. Hence, in this case wearing either a ruby or pearl would be contraindicated, as the circulatory system is already operating on a high level.

On the other hand, should your Sun be in opposition to the planet Saturn, wearing a ruby-sapphire combination would be useful and would counter the negative energy received at birth. Of special concern are aspects to the Sun, if one is male, and to the Moon, if one is female. Simply put, one would *not* wear a gemstone when the planet ruling it is well aspected, for such would not be needed.

ASTROLOGICAL HEALTH SYNTHESIS

Planet	Gemstone	Vitamin	Mineral	Gland	Rulership
Sun	Ruby	A, Paba, Pant. Ac.	Chromium	Thymus	Circulatory System
Moon	Pearl	B_6	Magnesium	Pancreas	Body Fluids
Mercury	Emerald	B_1, Folic Acid	Iodine	Thyroid	Respiratory/ Nervous System
Venus	Diamond	———	Copper	———	Venous Circulation
Mars	Coral	B_2, B_{12}, C, Niacin	Iron, Manganese	Adrenals, Gallbladder, Parathyroid	Skin, Muscles
Jupiter	Topaz	D, Biotin, Choline, Inositol, Lecithin	Selenium	Adrenal, Liver, Spleen	Arterial Circulation
Saturn	Sapphire	E	Zinc, Calcium, Sulphur		Skeletal System
Uranus	Lapis Lazuli	B Complex, Niacinamide	Potassium, Sodium	Pineal, Pituitary, Suprarenal	Sympathetic Nervous System
Neptune	Malachite	See Jupiter	———	Pituitary	Spinal Canal
Pluto	Citrine (smokey) Quartz	———	———	Gonads, Ovaries	Excretory System

Note: In the original astrological system as taught by the Indian astrologers, there were only seven planets. Uranus, Neptune, and Pluto were not yet discovered. These were later added to the system.

Besides the selection of the correct gemstone, one must also consider the size of the stone to be worn. In other words, the greater the affliction to a particular planet—that is, negative conjunctions, squares, and oppositions—the greater the size of the stone required to counter the negative influence. For instance, Saturn conjunct the Sun or Moon by itself would necessitate a smaller ruby or cat's eye than, say, this conjunction further squared or opposed by other planets. It is here that one is best advised to seek out an expert who can use radiesthesia to test various size stones to determine the best match.

Third, each stone selected must be properly mounted. This will enable its energy to transfer to the electromagnetic fields of the body. To do this each stone must be mounted so that it actually touches the skin underneath it. In other words, there should be no metal between the stone and the person wearing it. You should be able to look through the bottom of the ring and actually see the bottom of the gemstone. Unfortunately, many modern jewelers are totally unaware of this necessary crafting. As a result they produce rings that are aesthetically pleasing but metaphysically useless.

To gain the maximum effectiveness of this color talisman, you might also wish to pay attention to which finger a particular gemstone is worn on. While it is often commonplace to wear a ring on the fourth, or ring, finger, this may not be the best course of action. The ancients assigned each of the fingers to the planets as follows: thumb–Venus; first finger—Jupiter; second finger—Saturn; third finger—Sun; and fourth finger—Mercury.

Note that the so-called ring finger has been assigned rulership of the Sun. It is not by accident that this finger on the left hand—the hand closest to the heart—is where one normally wears a wedding ring. Astrologically speaking, the Sun rules the Sign Leo and the heart. Note, too, that the planets Mars and Moon have not been assigned to a particular phalange. Instead, they rule various mounts that lie below the fourth finger.

To understand what I am suggesting here, suppose your horoscope indicates that the planet Saturn is afflicted. To counter this negative influence you should be wearing a sapphire. Since Saturn rules the second finger, the sapphire should be worn there. As for whether it should be worn on the right or left hand, various, sometimes conflicting teachings suggest one or the other.

Generally, it is held that the left hand represents the talents we have been born with. The right hand suggests what we do with them. In recent years, students of muscle testing (a field known as applied kinesiology) have suggested that some watches and jewelry worn on the left hand weaken one's Vital Life Force. If you meet a student of this belief, don't be surprised if he or she is wearing a wedding ring and/or watch on the right hand and wrist.

Now, to further understand the magick of gemstones, let's look at the qualities of the stones themselves.

RUBY

Ruled by the Sun, the ruby has a grand and glorious history. It is said to be an emblem of beauty and elegance, able to soothe troubled spirits, drive away sadness and evil thoughts, and open doors for whatever one should desire.

Tradition holds that it will warn its wearer of coming misfortune by changing its color. Likewise, it will revert to its prior hue once disaster has passed. Medically, it is used for the treatment of the heart and circulatory system, and for headaches, indigestion, eye diseases, anemia, and various mental disorders.

The stone itself is a variety of corundum, an oxide of aluminum. It and the sapphire are among the most popular and costly of all the gemstones. The most rare are said to be "pigeon blood" red and the majority have various faults. The true ruby was originally called the oriental ruby and is a beautiful crimson or vermilion transparent stone. In hardness, the ruby is a 9, next to the diamond.

In Sanskrit, various names for the ruby are found suggesting that it was held in greater value by the Hindus than any other stone. For instance, it is called *ratnaraj*, meaning "king of precious stones," or *ratnanayaka,* "leader of precious stones." Indian tradition holds that it be worn on the left hand or left side of the body, placing it close to the heart over which it has rulership.

In India, the following means to judge the qualities of a ruby are suggested: If immersed in milk 100 times its weight, and the red rays break out in the milk, the stone is considered superior. Likewise, if in darkness, the ruby throws out the glow of the Sun. And if rubbed on another stone, only the stone will show signs of the rubbing.

Indian teachings also hold that, to be effective, the ruby should be at least 2½ carats in weight and be as flawless as possible.

Pliny is said to have been one of the earliest authors to state that wearing the lychnis, or star variety of ruby, brings about favors from persons in power or with authority.

In Myanmar (formerly Burma), where some of the most valued rubies in the world are found, the stone is considered sacred and is thought to bring success in battle owing to its Mars-like coloration. In ancient times, Burmese kings always included the ruby in their crown jewels. The largest Burmese ruby to reach the West weighed 1,184 carats.

Tradition holds that the ruby has the ability to rend a hole in the etheric body, should it be worn by someone who uses its power for evil ends.

A ruby should be set in a ring of gold mixed with copper on a Sunday, Monday, or Thursday. The stone must touch the skin, and before wearing should be immersed for some time in unboiled milk or water from the Ganges.

The ruby releases red cosmic rays, which can cure diseases in which the discharges are cold and thin, such as anemia and the common cold.

CAT'S EYE

Ruled by the Moon's south node (also called the Dragon's Tail or, in Indian astrology, Ketu) the cat's eye has a long-honored tradition as a gemstone with great magical powers. Some Arabs hold that wearing this stone can make its wearer invisible.

This gemstone belongs to the chrysoberyl family and possesses a hardness of 8½. Dark green varieties are known as alexandarites, while pale to green yellow stones are called chrysolites. The varying colors and luster of the stones is called a chatoyant effect, and is due to internal microscopic hollow channels in the stone itself. These gems are found mainly in Sri Lanka, Brazil, China, and the Mogok mines of Burma; the latter's gems are considered the highest quality.

Tradition holds that the stone will assist healing of such diseases as boils, cholera, dropsy, headache, indigestion, and severe asthma. In Syria, a sister of the cat's eye was called the eye of adad, and was believed to save the sight of anyone afflicted by smallpox if the stone was passed over his or her eyes occasionally.

In the East, wearing a cat's eye is said to bring happiness from one's children and wealth, which it is also believed will be restored by wearing the stone. As its magick is said to be quick in action, many suggest wearing it during and after a trial. One should not wear stones that are cracked or blemished, as such will bring bad luck. Especially bad is wearing a stone with a black dot or spot in it.

Indian tradition holds that the cat's eye should be placed in a ring of silver and be first worn on the little finger on a Thursday at midnight. The stone should be no less than 3 carats. It is also held that wearing this stone cures diseases caused by an excess of bile in the system and will strengthen the mind and heart.

The cat's eye is said to produce rays that correspond to the infrared spectrum and are often suggested in the treatment of chronic or potentially terminal illness.

ONYX

Ruled by Rahu (the Dragon's Head, or north node of the Moon), tradition holds that this stone was part of the breastplate of the Aaron in the Bible.

Also known by the name *gomed*, the onyx is found in nearly every color. Its hardness is 7½ and chemically it is a silicate of zirconium and crystals. Colors range from red or green to blue, yellow, orange, brown, and black. While the highest quality is said to come from Sri Lanka, the stone is also found in Australia (New South Wales), France, Russia, and Kashmir.

For whatever reason, wearing an onyx or zircon is said to bring variable luck. It will be decidedly lucky for some people and equally unlucky for others. Supposedly, those with the planet Uranus prominent in their horoscope charts will gain the most through wearing it.

It is said to help cure various and sundry diseases, including rheumatism, worms, hyperacidity, insomnia, suicidal tendencies, liver disease, glandular diseases, and constipation. It is also said to arrest hemorrhages and to render its wearer chaste, which might account for its lack of popularity today.

Indian philosophy holds that the onyx generates ultraviolet rays. It is also said to cause sleeplessness, quarrels, and evoke specters and ghosts. One Indian tradition holds that when worn by someone born in August, the stone will ensure marital fidelity.

If unblemished, wearing the gomed is said to bring safety and protection from one's most deadly enemies. Health, wealth, and prosperity will also follow its owner. Worn when hunting, it is believed to protect the wearer from wild animals. It will also shield one from wounds if worn during a battle. Placed in the mouth, it is said to stop bleeding. When heart trouble is caused by stomach disorders or mental aggravation, wearing an onyx is often recommended.

This stone should be mounted in a ring consisting of the alloy of eight metals or silver, and be worn on the middle finger. The weight should be not less than 6 carats.

PEARL

Ruled by the Moon, the pearl, or pretiosa margarita, is found more in poetry than in magical legends. Traditions hold it a symbol for purity, faith, and chastity and give it rulership over the thirtieth year of marriage.

A natural pearl is formed by a mollusk such as the oyster or mussel. Its chemical composition consists of a carbonate of chalk and a small quantity of organic substance. Its hardness is about 3½ to 4.

The luster of pearls varies greatly. Colors may be both black and white with tinges of yellow, blue, salmon pink, red, brown, and green. The rosier the sheen, the better the quality.

Chief sources of pearls include the Persian Gulf, Sri Lanka, Australia, Venezuela, Japan, the Red Sea, and the Pacific. Tuticorin (South India) was renowned for its pearls for many centuries.

According to the ancient Hindus, the pearl was found with four other magical stones in the necklace of the god Vishnu. The four other stones were the diamond, ruby, emerald, and sapphire. Similar traditions hold that each pearl has a special meaning according to its color. The golden pearl is symbolic of wealth; the white, idealism; the pink, beauty; the gray, thought; the red, health and energy; and the black, philosophy.

Christian legend holds that the angel Gabriel protects all those who carry the pearl. Yet another tradition holds that salvation descended into the body of Adam in the form of a pearl.

Pearls, like other stones, are said to lose their luster if worn by one who is dying. The ancient Romans counseled the wearing of pearls by young girls to ensure preservation of their virginity, as the stone was held sacred to the goddess Diana and the Moon. Among the Hindus, it is common for the bride to wear a nose ring of pearls during the marriage ceremony. This is believed to ensure a happy marriage and offer protection from widowhood.

A single grain, ground to fine powder and drunk in new milk, was held a cure for irritability. Pearls were also held to remove violence or anger and bring patience and peace of mind. According to the Indians, pearls may be used to treat diabetes, tuberculosis, fevers, dropsy, colic, bladder diseases, eye diseases, and various mental disorders.

The wearing of defective pearls is said to bring bad fortune, depending on the exact nature of the defect. A spot without luster, like a hole, is said to bring leprosy to the wearer. A spot like the eye of a fish will bring the loss of children. Pearls that generally lack luster are said to shorten one's life.

Pearls should be of 2, 4, 6, or 11 carats and be set in a silver ring on Monday or Thursday, but never Saturday. The ring should be first worn on a Monday morning in the bright half of the lunar month.

According to tradition, pearls release cold waves of orange color, and hence can cure diseases that arise from hot rays and fevers.

CORAL

Ruled by the planet Mars, coral has a grand history. Roman gladiators wore it in their helmets to protect them in battle. Coral strings were tied around the necks of their children to keep away the evil eye and to aid dentition. Would-be murderers are said to be dissuaded from their anticipated crimes of passion if they wear coral. Children who wear coral at night were held to be safeguarded from nightmares. Pilgrims to Mecca were advised to carry chaplets made from coral beads.

Coral consists of calcium carbonate with a little magnesium carbonate. It is found in all the shallow seas and is especially abundant in the Mediterranean and off the coasts of Japan. For the most part, coral consists of skeletal material of the coral polyp, forming a core or base for the animals, which cling together in colonies. Its hardness is 3½.

In ancient times, coral was held a charm against lightning, shipwreck, fire, and whirlwinds. Coral is said to change color if the wearer is sick and will recover its color when the person does. Among Italians, coral carved into various shapes is used to ward off the evil eye. In India, it is held to prevent evil spirits from occupying the body of the deceased.

While colors vary, different shades of red predominate. The darker red coral is held to stimulate and serve as a tonic for the bloodstream. It is said to correspond with the thirty-fifth marriage year. The lighter, angel-skin variety is believed to influence the astral and mental bodies. Coral is also believed to aid in dissolving calcium deposits in joints and bones. Black coral, though somewhat rare, is said to contain and hold negative energy and hence must be worn with great caution.

According to the Indians, some of the diseases that coral is useful in treating include blood disorders, hypertension (high blood pressure), anemia, bleeding, boils, sexual diseases, swollen joints, constipation, liver troubles, and nervous exhaustion. Psychologically, coral with its yellow cosmic rays is often prescribed for indolence, depression, and impatience.

Coral has also been held a particularly lucky stone for brides and is said to bring happiness to married women as well. Red coral, some believe, will protect women from both widowhood and evil spirits.

For best effectiveness, red coral should be set in a ring of gold mixed with copper. The stone should be no less than 6 carats and should purchased and set on a Monday, Tuesday, or Thursday. The ring should be worn for the first time one hour after sunrise on Tuesday, the day ruled by Mars, its Lord. Red coral should never be worn with emeralds, diamonds, blue sapphires, or cat's eyes.

TOPAZ

Ruled by the planet Jupiter and corresponding to blue cosmic rays, the topaz or moonstone has long been a favorite with mystics throughout the world.

In antiquity, it was held that wearing a topaz would render the wearer invulnerable. Christian tradition makes it a symbol for justice, true love, divine love, friendship, clemency, and temperance. It is said to dispel sadness or melancholy and to confer riches and honor. If used as a divining rod, it will lead to the discovery of hidden springs of water or veins of gold.

The very word *topaz* is a derivative of an ancient Sanskrit word, *topas,* meaning "heat." Its power was held to increase as the Moon increased in light, especially when it was in the Sign of Scorpio. Wearing a topaz was said to drive away night terrors, keep one safe during epidemics, calm passions, dispel fear of death, and provide a glimpse of the beyond.

Generally, the yellow variety of quartz is given the name *topaz*, although the true topaz is much rarer. The stone has a hardness of 8 and is a fluorosilicate of aluminum and natural crystals. Its color can range from yellow to sherry and may be found in Brazil, Scotland, Ireland, Japan, and Sri Lanka. It is said to correspond to the sixteenth year of marriage.

Friendship and fidelity are often said to be the topaz's key words. When used for medicinal purposes, it is helpful in the treatment of laryngitis, scarlet fever, chicken pox, candida (yeast infections), hysteria, nervous disorders, whooping cough, paralysis, premenstrual syndrome (PMS), and any glandular disorders.

An interesting Indian tradition is that if a suitable husband cannot be found for a young girl and she wears a topaz, she will marry quickly. Similarly, wearers of topazes will be blessed with children and grandchildren.

One should never wear a stone with cracks, however, as such is believed to invite thefts. Milky stones are believed to cause bodily injuries. Stones with black and white casts will cause one's cattle to become ill. Wearing a stone with red dots on it is said to destroy wealth.

Topaz gemstones should be set in gold on either Monday or Thursday, the day ruled by its Lord. Weight should be not less than 3 carats, but should never be 6, 11, or 15 carats. It should first be worn on the ring finger of the right hand on a Thursday morning during the bright half of the lunar month.

DIAMOND

Ruled by the planet Venus, the diamond is said to be a generator of indigo cosmic rays. Traditions hold this stone as a symbol of innocence, fidelity, constancy, and, of course, love in the highest sense of the word. The High Priest Aaron was held to have worn a diamond on his finger that turned black when the Jews sinned.

When worn on the left side, the diamond was believed to confer peace and serenity and protect one from wild animals, serpents, werewolves, and the dreaded incubi and succubi. It is also believed to make those who wear it faithful to their marriage vows, hence its traditional use as a wedding or engagement ring.

A diamond has a hardness of 10, making it the hardest gemstone known. It is composed of pure carbon. Tradition holds that its name is a corruption of the ancient Greek name for a mineral that meant "invincible." Its specific gravity is unusually constant and its refractive index is the highest of all gemstones.

The finest of diamonds are colorless, although the stone occurs in various faint shades of color, with blue-white regarded as the best. Diamonds were first obtained from the Golconda mines in India near the river Kistna. Later they were discovered in Brazil and then South Africa, which is now the major supplier.

To obtain its magical properties, only stones without flaws should be worn. Black or red dots on the stone, which give the impression of a drop of water, are held inauspicious. Wearing a stone with dots like the claws of a crow is said to bring death to the wearer, and should be avoided at all costs. Stones with other defects are said to cause various mental disturbances, disasters, and diseases.

Indian legends hold that diamonds have three sexes: male, female, and eunuch. The male is held to be the best; the female, second; and the eunuch, last. The male diamond is said to have six or eight angles and, if reflected on water, will produce the seven colors of the rainbow. It should be light in weight but look large, and have no lines or dots. The female diamond is round and long, and has dots and lines together with the other qualities of its male counterpart. Lastly, the eunuch diamond has only three angles that are turned and is round, large, and heavy in weight.

Women who wish to be blessed with sons should wear an unblemished white diamond with a slight black hue, according to the Hindus. Wearing a white diamond with a slight hue of red, which is called the Kshatriya Diamond, is held to make one brave, an able diplomat, and a political leader who will achieve great success in his career. Similarly, wearing a diamond with a yellow hue, called Vaishya, brings one wealth, respect, and the luxuries of life. A stone with a black hue (Shudra) is thought to bring wisdom, wealth, and success to its wearer.

Diamonds are said to make a person fearless, patient, pure, and the vessel of good manners. They are said to aid in the cure of those diseases which come from the simultaneous disturbance of the elements Air, Fire, and Water. These include eye troubles, nose and ear complaints, facial paralysis, and lung diseases including pneumonia, bronchitis, and asthma. As Venus rules the diamond, it will also be useful in the treatment of sterility, diabetes, uterine diseases, hernia, laziness, and drunkenness.

Finally, since diamonds are very expensive, a 1½-carat stone is recommended. It should be set in platinum or silver, and be worn on the little finger of the right hand. It should first be worn on a Friday (Venus's day) during the bright half of the lunar month. Tradition holds that a diamond should not be worn along with a ruby, red coral, or yellow sapphire.

SAPPHIRE

Ruled by the planet Saturn, a sapphire contains a concentration of violet cosmic rays. Magical tradition holds that this stone was used for the wand of Moses and the tablets upon which the Ten Commandments were engraved. Likewise, it was said to be the sixth stone in Aaron's breastplate. Legend holds that peace will accompany the wearing of this stone, which has long symbolized loyalty, justice, nobility, truth, and pure conscience.

Its very name comes from the Sanskrit and means "beloved of Saturn," suggesting qualities of strength and endurance. The stone has a hardness of 9, placing it next to the diamond.

The blue sapphire is said to be lucky for lovers. It is also believed that its powers will disappear if worn by an evil-minded person. Should the stone be flawed by white lines, wearing it is said to cause eye problems. A milky stone will bring poverty. Accidents may happen to one wearing a cracked stone, while double-colored stones bring success to one's enemies. Stones with depressions will bring boils and ulcers. Yet another tradition holds that a sapphire will change color as a warning to the wearer that someone is conspiring or threatening an attack.

Sapphires should be worn only after giving them a trial period during which time they are placed in one's home or carried in one's pocket or handbag. If the energy of the stone is suitable to its wearer, it will remove poverty and bring wealth, health, longevity, happiness, prosperity, and fame.

Since sapphires have often been favored by royalty and the Church, some hold they are under the co-rulership of the Sun. This is explained by the fact that all sapphires are affected by the action of radium, and in fact even change color from blue to green, and then to yellow.

Sapphires are said to vibrate to the Air element and rule over the human nervous system and the skin. Hence, some of the diseases they are useful for include leucoderma, neurosis, neuralgia, sciatica, epilepsy, cerebro-spinal meningitis, concussions, rheumatism, cramps, tumors, and kidney and bladder weakness. Nerve pains are said to be especially responsive to treatment by the sapphire's rays.

Since there are many imitations of sapphires made from glass, one way of testing the genuineness of a stone is to immerse it in milk for some time. If it is genuine, the milk will take on the color of the stone and appear blue. Glass cannot cause this to happen.

To be most effective, sapphires should be set in a ring of steel and be worn for the first time on Saturday, on the middle finger of the right hand, two hours before sunset. They should be at least 5 carats in weight.

EMERALD

Here we have a stone that corresponds to the green cosmic rays, the planet Mercury, and the cold Earth element. Tradition holds that a great emerald on which was engraved the Great and Sacred

Name adorned the Ephod of the High Priest as recorded in the Book of Exodus. It is held to be symbolic of inspiration and wisdom, and increases understanding, eloquence, and renown. It was further believed to free the spirits of those possessed and to aid in the procurement of fortune.

Said to correspond to the fifth year of marriage, the stone was also held to bring about faithfulness and the ability to see into the future, and to be a preventive against the evil eye, witchraft, and snakes.

So beautiful are really good green specimens, it is believed that by gazing at such a stone one can actually improve one's eyesight. The great Pliny ranked the emerald third after the diamond and pearl for its great magical powers and wrote of them that, "Neither dimness nor shade, nor yet the light of a candle, causes them to lose their luster."

Again, like many other gemstones, the stone was said to change color in the presence of deception and treachery, much as a ruby would in ill health, or a topaz with poison! A most interesting tradition holds that the emperor Nero used a large emerald cut in the form of a concave lens to watch gladiatorial contests as an aid to his shortsightedness. Still another tradition holds that if a serpent gazes upon an emerald, it will be blinded. A symbol of kindness and love, this stone was considered very lucky if given as a gift by a lover. It was also believed to cure and protect one from epilepsy and insanity. But if blemished, the stone was believed to cause injury to the wearer, as well as deprive him of happiness with his parents by affecting their wealth.

The emerald with its hardness of 7¾ is indeed one of the most costly of gemstones. For the most part it is a beautiful velvety green variety of beryl, a silicate of aluminum and beryllium, with its green color coming from a small percentage of chromic oxide.

Healthwise, the green cosmic ray of the emerald is suggested for blood pressure, ulcers, cancer, heart trouble, influenza, asthma, skin injuries (especially burning), and to gain weight.

One way of testing the genuineness of an emerald is to hold it before the eyes. If it is real, it will cool the eyes. If it is simply glass, the eyes will become hot.

According to tradition, the emerald should be set in a silver ring on Wednesday. It should be worn for the first time on the little finger of the right hand, about two hours after sunrise, on a Wednesday (the day ruled by Mercury) in the bright half of the lunar month. Its weight should be no less than 3 carats. It should never be worn with red coral, a pearl, or a yellow sapphire.

ADDITIONAL STONES

The foregoing stones were the only ones assigned by the Ancients to the original hierarchy of planetary rulers, since only nine planets were then known to exist. With the discovery of the planets Uranus, Neptune, and Pluto, however, additional gemstones have also become important, although far less is known of their influence.

Lapis Lazuli

Ruled by the planet Uranus and the astrological sign Aquarius (Air), this stone has long been held as an aid to the development of clairvoyance and cosmic consciousness. One authority suggests that the stone was first used in Atlantis and that it "encompasses the universal principle of absolute light" as emitted from Venus, the lower octave of Uranus.

As such, it is said to stabilize the human vibration while at the same time opening up the various chakras, or psychic centers. This it can do since the minerals from which it is composed—mainly sodium, aluminum, silica, and sulfur—serve as atomic sensors. It is suggested that one should choose a stone that has bright, brilliant hues of blue if being used for meditative purposes. For physical health, stones with darker hues are suggested.

Ancient traditions hold that the stone confers love, tenderness, gentleness, fidelity, and simplicity of heart. Lazurite, another name for this stone, is a massive stone whose color ranges from azure blue through violet or greenish blue. Its hardness is 5 to 5½ and it often contains small grains of pyrite.

The world-renowned psychic Edgar Cayce often recommended this stone in his readings to improve mental, physical, and spiritual conditions, and to make the body "more sensitive to the higher vibrations." Traditions universally recommend wearing the stone for love and luck.

In ancient Egypt, pieces of lapis lazuli were regularly inscribed with various chapters of the *Book of the Dead,* which gives specific instructions for the passage of the soul through the underworld. A powerful amulet often recommended took the form of an eye crafted out of lapis and decorated with pure gold. Offerings of all things "good and holy" were instructed to be made before this symbolic eye, which legend held the supreme god Ra placed upon his head. A seal of it was supposed to "possess a god who will rejoice in its owner."

Yet another tradition holds that this stone was the fifth or the eleventh stone of the magic breastplate. Similarly, still another tradition claims that this stone, and not the emerald, was used on which to engrave the Ten Commandments. Some authorities consider lapis the sister stone of the sapphire, as it symbolizes the earth mother and sapphire the sky father.

Remembering that the Egyptian pharaoh often married his eldest sister, lapis was more than intimately associated with the Egyptian royal family. A strange correlation to this idea is a tradition that wearing this stone will cure the ill effects of incest.

In ancient times, physicians used the gem to treat eye problems, while learned alchemists often called it the "stone of Heaven."

Unfortunately, no instructions have been found as to the suggested weight of the stone to be worn, or the metal in which it should be set. One unusual Cayce reading, however, recommended its being encased in clear glass to reduce its radiations and placing it in sunlight for at least three hours before wearing.

Malachite

This stone is ruled by Pluto and the element Water. Its hardness is 3.5 to 4, and its color bright green, owing to its unusually high copper content (hydrated copper carbonate).

As early as 4000 B.C., the ancient Egyptians extracted malachite from various mines between Suez and the Sinai. It was held by them to be useful in the treatment of cholera and rheumatism.

Malachite is also a symbolic stone for the Moslem religion, where it is often used for the decoration of mosques. In the Middle Ages, it was a protection against the evil eye, an optical cure, a teething aid, and an insurer for safe and easy childbirth. Other traditions hold that it promotes tranquillity, prevents litigation, and brings success in business. It is also said to be symbolic of hope.

While its modern name was derived from the Greek *malache,* meaning "marsh mallow," whose soft green leaves it resembled, it is thought by some to be the "Lapis Liguris" often referred to in the Edgar Cayce readings.

Edgar Cayce called the action of this stone "atomic," and said that it combined "the radial activity of radium with the strengthening influences of gold and silver." Other authorities claim its primary action consists of the alignment of the crown chakra and stimulation of the pineal and pituitary glands.

Wearing this gem is said to stimulate the optic nerve, thereby producing cones, as well as aiding the functions of the pancreas and the spleen. Because of its influence on the pancreas, it is held useful in the treatment of cataracts and abnormal blood sugar levels.

Unfortunately, no recommendations as to its weight or setting are known. My personal choice would be gold. Being a higher octave of the planet, Mars, Tuesday would be the best day to commence its wearing.

Opal

Here we find a stone ruled by Neptune and the element Water. It has a hardness of 6, and is available in a wide array of colors, including the somewhat rare black opal.

Originally found in such diverse locations as Mexico, Arabia, Sri Lanka, Ireland, and Czechoslovakia, opals are now mostly exported from Australia. Most opals contain some kind of milky appearance owing to cloudy inclusions which produce rainbow effects. Only the so-called fire opal from Mexico, with its orange or red coloring, is predominantly clear. Even the legendary black opal contains some gray or blue in the background. The stone itself is composed of silica, like quartz, but with various amounts of water.

Since ancient times it has best been described by a single word— *magick*! According to Pliny, "the opal is made up of the glories of the most precious gems which make description so difficult. For amongst them is the gentler fire of the ruby, the rich purple of the amethyst, the sea-green of the emerald, glittering together in union indescribable."

It has been likened to a tear fallen from the Moon, a rainbow veiled in white vapor, or the stars of many colors shining in the Milky Way. Although it is often spoken of as the "Child of Love," if one's lover is false, its influence will be reversed. An illustration of this is the belief that King Alfonso XII of Spain gave his wife an opal at their wedding and she died soon afterwards. When the same stone was then presented to his sister-in-law, she too passed away within three months.

One tradition holds that whoever carries it can acquire the art of invisibility, hence its use by thieves. In the presence of poison, it was believed it would turn pale. It would also change color should one come in contact with a secret enemy, but blush with joy in the presence of a secret lover.

To the ancients, the opal symbolized children, friendships, feelings, tears, prayers, and the grace of pardon, and it was believed to increase fidelity. If held between one's eyes, it was said to direct one's thoughts. Held in the left hand and gazed upon, it was held to grant one's deepest desires. Because of its connection with Neptune, it has long been associated with visions, the sea and all liquids, narcotics, and "other world" experiences. One Indian tradition holds that the opal makes one religious and increases one's faith in God.

Since it is formed through the decomposition of various rock ingredients, opals are often found in volcanic lavas or in veins in sandstone. Should the stone be overheated to the point of becoming lifeless, its vitality can be revived by bathing it in oil for a few hours, which is an unusual quality it shares only with amber.

The very word *opal* comes from the Sanskrit *upala,* meaning "precious," which I guess says it all! Still another tradition holds it an aid to the development of ESP and clairvoyance. Its use as a medical amulet is also not uncommon.

One authority holds that its influence is so powerful that it can influence all of the chakras, depending on the particular shades it contains. For instance, opals containing golden orange, green violet, and blue are said to influence the crown chakra. The black opal containing blues, violets, and greens affects the brow center, while green and gold fires affect the throat center. Lighter shades, such as white with orange and red and green flashes, influence the heart center; pale blues and violets, the solar plexus center; and golden red fire and cherry, the spleen and sacral centers.

A word of warning. Opals should never be mounted in the same setting with emeralds, lapis lazuli, rubies, sapphires, or garnets. Because of its affinity with Neptune, silver is said to be the most desirable metal for its setting. And since Neptune is the higher octave of Mercury, Wednesday would be the best day to first wear such a stone.

All gemstones work through the magic of their various colors and shades, which transmit vibrations that alter the electromagnetic fields of what we call the auric and etheric bodies, about which we sadly know very little. It is indeed unfortunate that the genuine occult teaching in regard to the use of gemstones has deteriorated to the point at which they are simply assigned to a particular astrological sign.

Likewise, if one is fortunate enough to have selected the correct stone, one must be certain that it is properly mounted so that its projected energy may reach out. Many times I have seen the correct stone either wrongly combined with other stones or improperly mounted, so that it is relegated to being nothing more than a costly decoration. Certainly it is not the fault of the stone when this occurs.

What better way to conclude this chapter than by sharing this list of gemstones that tradition long ago assigned to the Twelve Apostles. When and where this list first appeared is unknown even to Zolar. It is said than anyone who wishes to acquire the characteristics or spiritual qualities of a particular disciple may do so by wearing his stone, after it has been properly consecrated.

St. Peter—Jasper
St. James—Chalcedony
St. John—Emerald
St. Matthew—Amethyst
St. Mark—Beryl
St. Simon—Sardius
St. Andrew—Sapphire
St. James the Lesser—Topaz
St. Philip—Sardonyx
St. Bartholomew—Jacinth
St. Thaddaeus—Chrysoprase
St. Mattias—Chrysolite

12

The Color Magick of Flowers and Shrubs

★ ★ ★
★ ★
★ ★

And why take ye thought for raiment? Consider the lilies of the field, how they grow: they toil not, neither do they spin: And yet I say unto you, That even Solomon in all his glory was not arrayed like one of these.

(MATTHEW 7:28–29)

Certainly no discussion of color would be complete without at least a brief mention of the ancient traditions surrounding flowers. While many persons may never have the opportunity to experience the magick of owning a gemstone, few have not stood in awe before God's handiwork.

Essentially, the dominant color of each flower serves as its symbolic indication. White signifies purity, virginity, and innocence. Reds, running from the bright color of Mars to the soft blush, signify passion, desire, guilt, shame, and, of course, modesty, youth, and tender love. Yellows indicate wealth, prosperity, generosity, thoughtfulness, and so on. Blues indicate wisdom, piety, religious feelings, and general spirituality. Purples signify power, greatness, ambition, and essentially the "Higher Path." Green signifies growth, hope, and the very essence of life.

Of course, there are no really black flowers, which would signify death and transition if they could be found. The fact that they cannot suggests that what we call death is simply a grand illusion or transition, which is in keeping with esoteric teachings worldwide.

Besides the general assignment of flowers according to color, various legends pertain to the existence of a language, or hidden meaning, that accompanies each one. Following is an abbreviated list of such traditions, which will make clear how one's apparently random choice of flowers and shrubs may be viewed as a unique form of divination.

Acacia (white)—Pure or chaste love
Aconite (wolfsbane)—Protection
Agnus Castus—Coldness
Almond—Deception, indiscretion
Aloe—Grief, strife
Amaranth—Immortality, eternal devotion
Angelica—Inspiration, pure thought
Apple—Fortune
Auricula—Seduction
Azalea—Happiness, temperance
Bachelor's Button—Single blessedness
Balm—Spiritual strength
Balsam—Impatience
Barberry—Ill temper
Basil—Hatred, disdain
Begonia—Cold, dark thoughts
Belladonna—Silent coquetry
Betony—Surprise friendship
Blue Bell—Constancy, fidelity
Borage—Bluntness
Broom—Humility
Buttercup—Ingratitude, mockery of wealth

Cactus—Warmth
Camomile—Submission to one's adversary
Carnation (red)—Kisses for my wounded heart
Cedar—Enduring strength
Centaury—Felicity
Cherry—Sound education
Chestnut—Luxury
Chrysanthemum (red)—Love forlorn
Chrysanthemum (yellow)—Love slighted
Chrysanthemum (white)—Truth
Clematis—Devotion, idealistic beauty
Cock's Comb—Impatience
Colocynth—Bitterness
Columbine—Folly, gaiety
Convolvulus—Separation, uncertainty
Coriander—Merit concealed
Crocus—Feelings
Cyclamen—Jealousy, diffidence
Cypress—Despair, mourning
Daffodil—High regard
Dahlia—False abundance, instability
Daisy (white)—Youth, innocence
Dandelion—Oracle of the future
Daphne—Amorous curiosity
Daylily—Coquetry
Dog's Tooth Violet—Grand deceit
Dragonwort—Terror
Ebony—Impatience
Elder—Moroseness
Elm—Dignity
Euphorbia—Love
Evergreen—Poverty
Fennel—Praiseworthy
Fig—Great sweetness
Flax—Protector
Fleur-de-Lis—Flame

Fly Trap—Deceit
Forget-Me-Not—True love
Foxglove—Insincerity
Fuchsia—Taste
Gardenia—Homage
Gentian—Bitterness
Geranium (scarlet)—Tenderness, affection
Gilliflower—Constancy
Gladiola—Character strength
Goldenrod—Encouragement, joy
Grape (wild)—Charity
Hawthorne—Prudence, hope
Hazel—Pardon, reconciliation
Hellebore—Scandal
Hemlock—Death, treason
Hemp—One's fate
Hollyhock—Simplicity, fecundity
Honeysuckle—Sweetness
Hortensia—Uncertainty
Hyacinth (purple)—Sorrow, tears
Hydrangea—Heartlessness
Hyssop—Heart's mystery
Iris—Tender love, message
Ivy—Marriage, attachment
Ixia—Eternal love
Jasmine—Love's delight
Jonquil—Languor
Juniper—Protection
Larkspur—Lightness, carelessness
Laurel—Honors, glory
Lavender—Mystery, distrust
Lilac—First love
Lily of the Valley—Happiness returned, beauty
Lobelia—Malevolence
Locust—Elegance
Lotus—Love estranged

Magnolia—Generosity
Maidenhair—Discretion
Mallow—Sweet sorrow
Maple—Wisdom
Marigold—Despair, sadness
Mimosa—Sensitive love
Mint—Virtue
Mistletoe—Overcome difficulties
Morning Glory—Affectation
Mulberry—Prudent wisdom
Myrtle—Protection
Narcissus—Egotism
Nasturtium—Patriotism
Nettle—Cruelty, evil actions
Nightshade—Falsehood
Oak Leaves—Bravery
Oleander—Beware
Olive—Peace
Orange—Virginal purity
Orchis—Faith
Palm—Victorious
Pansy—Thoughts
Parsley—Festivity
Passion Flower—Suffering
Peach—Unequaled charms
Pear—Affection, betrothals
Pelargonium (white)—Eagerness
Peony—Regrets, bashfulness
Periwinkle (blue)—Friendship
Petunia—An intercepted message
Phlox—Arduous love
Pine—Pity
Pomegranate—Folly
Poppy—Silence
Primrose—Youth, first love
Ranunculus—Ingratitude, treachery

Raspberry—Remorse
Rose—Love
Rosemary—Remembrance
Saffron—Dangerous success
Sainfoin—Stirred up emotions
Saxifrage—Disdain
Scabious—Unfortunate infatuation
Scilla—Emotional detachment
Shamrock—Light-heartedness
Snapdragon—Presumption
Snowdrop—Hope
Star of Bethlehem—Purity
Strawberry—Foresight
Sunflower—Gratitude
Sweet William—Gallantry
Sycamore—Curiosity
Thistle—Austerity
Thorn Apple—Deceit, disquietude
Thyme—Activity
Tulip (red)—Declaration of love
Valerian—Heart's wound
Veronica—Fidelity
Vervain—Enchantment
Vine—Intoxication
Violet—Modesty, faithfulness
Waterlily—Purity of heart
Weeping Willow—Mourning
White Jasmine—Amiability
Witch Hazel—A spell, enchantment
Wormwood—Absence
Yew—Sorrow
Zinnia—Thoughts of absent friends

No discussion of flowers would be complete without brief mention of the very popular Bach Flower Remedies. Of the various homeopathic remedies that have come into use in recent years, the Bach are perhaps the best known.

Although strictly speaking, these popular remedies are not actually prepared homeopathically by dilution and succussion, they have nonetheless been categorized as homeopathic by the FDA. Discovered by Dr. Edward Bach (pronounced *batch,* as in "batchelor" or *baych* as in "bay") as a safe alternative to regular homeopathic remedies or allopathic drugs, they are dispensed according to the mental state of the recipient rather than the nature of the disease.

It was Dr. Bach's belief that all illness results, not from germs or bacteria, but rather from a "conflict between Soul and Mind." When a soul is led astray from its true purpose, a conflict arises that, if unresolved, will result in physical illness. Hence, what is called disease has as its object the bringing back of the personality to the Divine Will of the soul. Faulty thought patterns, then—not bacteria and germs—cause illness. According to Bach, "Disease is the result of wrong thinking and wrong doing, and ceases when the act and thought are put in order."

To bring about this reordering, Bach was psychically led to the selection of some thirty-eight flower essences that would alter those mental states. He grouped his flower essences into the following broad categories: Fear, uncertainty, lack of interest in present circumstances, loneliness, oversensitivity, despondency or despair, and overcare for the welfare of others.

Although Bach did not categorize his remedies by color, his teachings are best illustrated in a poster of the Flower Essences distributed by the Bach Foundation. (See Appendix B). The following is a summation of those correspondences:

Color	Gem	Flower Remedy	

OVERCARE

Red	Ruby	Beech	Vervain
		Chicory	Vine
		Rockwater	

FEAR

Blue	Moonstone	Aspen	Red Chestnut
		Cherry Plum	Rock Rose
		Mimulus	

LONELINESS

Yellow	Coral	Heather	Water Violet
		Impatiens	

DESPONDENCY/DESPAIR

Orange	Pearl	Crabapple	Pine
		Elm	Star of Bethlehem
		Larch	Sweet Chestnut
		Oak	Willow

OVERSENSITIVITY

Green	Emerald	Agrimony	Holly
		Centaury	Walnut

LACK OF INTEREST

Violet	Sapphire	Chestnut Bud	Olive
		Clematis	White Chestnut
		Honeysuckle	Wild Rose
		Mustard	

UNCERTAINTY

Indigo	Diamond	Cerato	Hornabeam
		Gentian	Scleranthus
		Gorse	Wild Oat

Bach's remedies are another example of the wonderful healing power of color, in yet another form. Readers whose taste buds have been titillated by our brief discussion of Dr. Bach's work should consult Appendix B for further references.

Now, what better way to end this chapter than to recall the words of the Bard, Alfred, Lord Tennyson:

> *Flower in the crannied wall,*
> *I pluck you out of the crannies,*
> *I hold you here root and all, in my hand,*
> *Little flower—but if I could understand*
> *What you are, root and all, and all in all,*
> *I should know what God and man is.*
> "Flower in the Crannied Wall," 1869

13

Putting It into Practice

> *Disease is solely and purely corrective: it is neither vindictive nor cruel: but it is the means adopted by our own Souls to point out to us our faults: to prevent our making greater errors: to hinder us from doing more harm: and to bring us back to that path of Truth and Light from which we have strayed.*
>
> —DR. EDWARD BACH, *Heal Thyself*

We are nearing the end of our journey through the magick of color. I hope everyone reading these words has begun to think in technicolor, which is in keeping with the intentions of the Grand Architect who freely gave us green grass, blue skies, and the flowers of the field. When it comes to disease, however, few of us have been wise enough to see its manifestation—not as a curse, but as a true blessing enabling us to return to our spiritual compass in order to chart a new course based on our unique path of truth.

Through the use of the pendulum, with a little practice, you can easily ascertain which colors are useful in treating a particular problem. However, it is sometimes helpful to have a list of major problems and their color solutions at your fingertips. These colors can then be tested and, if found useful, put into immediate practice. The following has been compiled from various sources. To make it quick and easy to use, I have coded the colors as follows: red (R), orange (O), yellow (Y), green (G), blue (B), indigo (I), violet (V), ultraviolet (UV), infrared (IR), lemon (L), turquoise (T), purple (P), magenta (M), and scarlet (S).

MAJOR PROBLEMS AND THEIR COLOR SOLUTIONS

Abscess: G-I-O-Y (with Fever, B)
Adrenals: L-S-G
Alcoholism (chronic): B-M-S-O
Allergies: L-Y-O
Alopecia: O-L-M
Anemia: G-Y-I-R-L
Angina: L-M-P
Anorexia: G-M-Y
Appetite (loss): G-B
Arteriosclerosis: L-P-M
Asthma: During attack, P-S-O; between attacks, L-O-M
Bad breath: L
Black eye: I-O-L
Bleeding: V
Blood pressure (high): L-P-M-I
Blood pressure (low): L-S-M
Boils: O
Bone fractures: after setting fracture, O-L-B
Bronchitis: Acute, T-V-P; chronic, L-B-V-P
Bruises: I-O-L
Burns: B-I-T-G
Bursitis: Acute, G-B-I; chronic, L-O-B
Candida (thrush): T
Canker sores: G-B-I-V
Cataract: L-M
Chicken pox: G-B-I
Cigarette smoking: G-O-L

Circulation (poor): R
Cold: Common, G-B, chronic, L
Colitis: G-Y-I
Constipation: L-Y-O
Cough: L-B-G
Cuts: I-T-G-M
Cystitis: G-I
Deafness: L
Diabetes: L-G-Y-M
Diarrhea: Y-T-I
Earache: T-O-V
Eczema: T-I-L-O
Emphysema: L-O-Y
Endometriosis: L-M-P-I
Extraction, tooth: P-T-I
Farsightedness: L-Y-O-R
Flatulence: O
Flu: G-B-M-P
Food poisoning: Contact nearest Poison Control Center, then
   G-M
Fever (cause unknown): G-B-M-P
Gallstones: L-O
Gastritis: O-T-I
Glaucoma: L-I-M
Gout: L-M-S
Gum disease: T-L-I
Hayfever: L-T-B
Headache: V-P
Hemorrhoids: L-I
Hepatitis: Acute, G-B-R; chronic, L-R-M-I
Hernia: L-Y-I
Hiccough: O-I
Hypothyroid: L-I-G-P
Hysteria: B-M-G-S
Immune deficiency: R-L-Y-V
Impotency: G-O-M-S

Indigestion: O
Insomnia: V-P
Jaundice: L-R-Y-M
Kidney stones: L-M
Laryngitis: Acute, T-V; chronic, L-B
Lead poisoning: L
Leukemia: R-L-M-I
Liver (cirrhosis): L-R-M-I
Low blood sugar: L-V
Measles: G-B-I
Memory (poor): V
Menopause: G-M
Menstrual cycle: Absent, Y-L-G-S-M; irregular, I
Migraine: P-S
Miscarriage (tendency to): G-I
Mononucleosis: L-Y-T
Nasal catarrh: G-B-S
Nearsightedness: L-Y-O-R
Neuralgia: T-I
Nosebleed: I
Obesity: L-O-G-S
Osteoporosis: O-L-M-Y
Pain (to alleviate): I-V-P
Pancreatitis: Acute, T-B-I-M; chronic, L
Parkinson's: L-Y-O
Phlebitis: L-P-M-S
Pinworms: Y-B
Pleurisy: Acute, G-B-I-M-V; chronic, L-I
Pneumonia: G-B-M-S-P
Prostate: L-O-I
Sciatica: T-I
Shingles: Acute, G-I; chronic, V
Skin diseases: T-I-L-O
Sore throat: S-G-B
Sterility: G-O-M-S
Stress (emotional): V-P

Sunstroke: B-P
Tachycardia: T-M-S
Tics (nervous): V-M-O
Tinnitus: L-Y-O-R
Toothache: I
Tooth extraction: Before, P; after, T-I
Ulcers (stomach): L-I
Vertigo: G-P

Important Note: Remember that color therapy is complementary, rather than an alternative, to one's regular health care. Be sure to consult your primary health-care professional whenever the need arises.

POSTSCRIPT

I often wonder when I begin writing a new book how I will know that it is really done. When have I said all that needs to be told? My painter friends tell me they have the very same problem. Once a canvas is seemingly complete, there is always the feeling that they should go back and add another stroke, a splash of color here and there.

In retrospect, I guess the problem stems from the fact that both paintings and books really create themselves. The author and the artist are simply media through which the creative process takes place. It's simply a matter of getting out of the way and letting the Creator create.

By now I must assume that I have made at least a partial case for your thinking in color. Our task, then, is to understand why this is so, and to use our newfound knowledge for the benefit of ourselves, our families, and humanity. Perhaps the Good Book says it best.

> Study to shew thyself approved unto God, a workman that needeth not to be ashamed, rightly dividing the word of truth.
>
> (II Timothy 2:15)

APPENDIX A:
THE THERAPEUTIC VALUE
OF LIGHT AND COLOR*

Kate W. Baldwin, M.D., Former Senior Surgeon,
Woman's Hospital, Philadelphia

In the effort to obtain relief from suffering, many of the more
simple but potent measures have been overlooked while we have
grasped at the obscure and complicated.

Sunlight is the basic source of all life and energy upon earth.
Deprive plant or animal life of light, and it soon shows the lack
and ceases to develop. Place a seed in the very best of soil or a
human being in a palace, shut out the light, and what happens?
Without food (in the usual sense of the term) man can live many
days; without liquids a much shorter time; but not at all without
the atmosphere which surrounds him at all times and to which

*From a paper presented to the Medical Society of the State of Pennsylvania,
October 12, 1926.

he pays so little attention. The forces on which life mostly depends are placed nearly or quite beyond personal control.

For centuries scientists have devoted untiring effort to discover means for the relief or cure of human ills and restoration of the normal functions. Yet in neglected light and color there is a potency far beyond that of drugs and serums.

In order that the whole body may function perfectly, each organ must be a hundred per cent perfect. When the spleen, the liver, or any other organ falls below normal, it simply means that the body laboratories have not provided the required materials with which to work, either because they are not functioning, as a result of some disorder of the internal mechanism, or because they have not been provided with the necessary materials. Before the body can appropriate the required elements, they must be separated from the waste matter.

Each element gives off a characteristic color wave. The prevailing color wave of hydrogen is red, and that of oxygen is blue, and each element in turn gives off its own special color wave. Sunlight, as it is received by the body, is split into the prismatic colors and combinations, as white light is split by passage through a prism. Everything on the red side of the spectrum is more or less stimulating, while the blue is sedative.

There are many shades of each color, and each is produced by a little different wave length. Just as sound waves are turned to each other and produce harmony or discords, so color waves may be tuned, and only so can they be depended on always to produce the same results.

If one requires a dose of castor oil, he does not go to a drug store and request a little portion from each bottle on the shelves. I see no virtue, then, in the use of the whole white light as a therapeutic measure when the different colors can give what is required without taxing the body to rid itself of that for which it has no use, and which may do more or less harm.

If the body is sick it should be restored with the least possible effort. There is no more accurate or easier way than by giving the color representing the lacking element, and the body will, through its radioactive forces, appropriate them and so restore the normal balance. Color is the simplest and most accurate therapeutic measure yet developed.

For about six years I have given close attention to the action of colors in restoring body functions, and I am perfectly honest in saying that, after nearly thirty-seven years of active hospital practice and private practice in medicine and surgery, I can produce quicker and more accurate results with colors than with any or all other methods combined—and with less strain on the patient.

In many cases, the functions have been restored after the classical remedies have failed. Of course, surgery is necessary in some cases, but results will be quicker and better if color is used before and after operation. Sprains, bruises and traumata of all sorts respond to color as to no other treatment. Septic conditions yield, regardless of the specific organism. Cardiac lesions, asthma, hay fever, pneumonia, inflammatory conditions of the eyes, corneal ulcers, glaucoma, and cataracts are relieved by the treatment.

The treatment of carbuncles with color is easy compared to the classical methods. One woman with a carbuncle involving the back of the neck from mastoid to mastoid, and from occipital ridge to the first dorsal vertebra, came under color therapy after ten days of the very best of attention. From the first day of color application, no opiates, not even sedatives, were required. This patient was saved much suffering, and she has little scar.

The use of color in the treatment of burns is well-worth investigating by every member of the profession. In such cases the burning sensation caused by the destructive forces may be counteracted in from twenty to thirty minutes, and does not return. True burns are caused by the destructive action of the red side of the spectrum, hydrogen predominating. Apply oxygen by the use of the blue side of the spectrum, and much will done to relieve the nervous strain, the healing processes are rapid, and the resulting tissues soft and flexible.

In very extensive burns in a child of eight years of age there was almost complete suppression of urine for more than 48 hours, with a temperature of 105 to 106 degrees. Fluids were forced to no effect, and a more hopeless case is seldom seen. Scarlet was applied just over the kidneys at a distance of eighteen inches for twenty minutes, all other areas being covered. Two hours later, the child voided eight ounces of urine.

In some unusual and extreme cases that had not responded to other treatment, normal functioning has been restored by color therapy. At present, therefore, I do not feel justified in refusing any case without a trial. Even in cases where death is inevitable, much comfort may be secured.

There is no question that light and color are important therapeutic media, and that their adoption will be of advantage to both the profession and the people.

APPENDIX B:
SOURCES AND SUPPLIERS

Following is a list of suppliers and organizations mentioned in this work that welcome inquiries from readers. Please mention Zolar when you write or call, and be sure to enclose a self-addressed, stamped envelope for easy reply.

GENERAL INFORMATION AND RESEARCH ON COLOR

The best single source for the latest developments in color therapy and research. Publishes periodic newsletter, various books on color:

DINSHAH HEALTH SOCIETY (NONPROFIT)
100 Dinshah Drive
Malaga NJ 08328
(609) 692-4686

PENDULUMS

The following suppliers offer professional pendulums in a wide variety of styles and materials, including those custom tuned to the user. Write or call them for catalogs, price lists:

BRUCE COPEN LABORATORIES (USA/CANADA)
Psitech
POB 291
Wadsworth IL 60083
(1-800) 726-1880

BRUCE COPEN LABORATORIES (UK)
Highfield Dane Hill
Haywards Heath Sussex RH17 7EX
England
0825-790214

AMERICAN SOCIETY OF DOWSERS, INC.
Bookstore
101 Railroad Street
St Johnsbury VT 05819
(802) 748-8565

SAMUEL WEISER, INC.
132 E. 24th Street
New York NY 10010
(212) 777-6363

APPENDIX B

COLOR PROJECTORS

Plans to build your own inexpensive projector:

DINSHAH HEALTH SOCIETY
(See General Information)

Miniature Fresnel Projector (Order projector, 12 slide holders, and bulb):

TIMES SQUARE LIGHTING
318 W. 47th Street
New York NY 10036
(212) 245-4155

PLASTIC GELS AND COLOR FILTERS

Most large cities have a theatrical materials supplier; look in the phone book yellow pages. One of these dealers is:

SAMARCO
P.O. Box 153008
Dallas TX 75215
(214) 421-0757

COLOR HEALING CORRESPONDENCE COURSE

Leads to a diploma in Color Healing and psychology:

BRANTRIDGE FOREST SCHOOL (UK)
Highfield, Dane Hill
Haywards Heath Sussex RH17 7EX
England
0825-790214

SUSSEX COLLEGE OF TECHNOLOGY (USA)
7 Waterfront Plaza
500 Alamoana #400
Honolulu HI 96813
(708) 217-1880

COLORONIC (NONLUMINOUS) INSTRUMENT

Special easy-to-use device uses magnetic color frequencies, rather than projecting actual light. Unique device:

BRUCE COPEN LABS
(See Pendulums)

COLOR THERAPY EYEWEAR

Brand new. A fast, easy way to channel color into the body through the eyes. Comes as complete set of seven colored eyeglasses to be worn or clipped on:

TOOLS FOR EXPLORATION
4460 Redwood Highway, Suite 2
San Rafael CA 94903
(1-800) 456-9887

ASTROLOGICAL CHARTS

For accurately calculated horoscope charts:

CAROL JEPSON
420 E. 64th Street
New York NY 10021
(212) 758-4887

BACH FLOWER INFORMATION

For books, writings, and remedies of Edward Bach:

ELLON BACH USA, INC.
644 Merrick Road
Lynbrook NY 11563-9668
(516) 593-2206 or (1-800) 433-7523

FURTHER READING

These fine books are just a few of those available for further study of the High Magick of Color.

Bannerman-Philips, E. Ivy A. *Amulets and Birthstones*. Los Angeles: Llewellyn Publications, 1950.

Barnard, Julian, ed. *Collected Writings of Edward Bach*. Hereford, UK: Bach Education Programme, 1987.

Bhattacharyya, A. K. *Gem Therapy*. Calcutta: Firma KLM Private Ltd, 1976.

———. *Science of Cosmic Ray Therapy*. Calcutta: Firma KLM Private Ltd, 1976.

———. *Teletherapy*. Calcutta: Firma KLM Private Ltd, 1977.

Birren, Faber. *Color: A Survey in Words and Pictures*. New Hyde Park, NY: University Books Inc, 1963.

Buckland, Raymond. *Practical Candle Burning Rituals*. St. Paul, MN: Llewellyn, 1984.

———. *Candle Burning Rituals*. Kent, UK: New Age Fellowship, Finbarr Inter, 1983.

Clark, Linda. *The Ancient Art of Color Therapy*. New York: Pocket Books, 1978.

———. *Color Healing, an Exhaustive Survey*. Mokelumne Hill, CA: Health Research, 1956.

Copen, Bruce. *A Rainbow of Health*. W. Sussex, UK: Academic Publications, 1975.

———. *Magic of the Aura*. W. Sussex, UK: Academic Publications, 1974.

Crow, W. B., *Precious Stones*. Wellingborough, Northamptonshire, UK: The Aquarian Press, 1968.

de Laurence, L. W. *The Great Book of Magical Art*. Chicago: de Laurence Co, 1915.

Dinshah, Darius. *Let There Be Light*. Malaga, NJ: Dinshah Health Society, 1985.

———. *The Spectro-Chrome System*. Malaga, NJ: Dinshah Health Society, 1979.

George, Llewellyn. *Perpetual Planetary Hour Book*. Los Angeles: Llewellyn Publications, 1906.

Gimbel, Theo. *Healing Through Colour*. Saffron Walden, UK: C. W. Daniel Co Ltd, 1980.

Hills, Norah. *You Are a Rainbow*. Boulder Creek, CA: University of the Trees Press, 1979.

Hunt, Roland. *The Seven Keys to Colour Healing*. London: C. W. Daniel Co Ltd, 1971.

Jaegers, Beverly. *Secrets of the Aura*. Jerome, AZ: Luminary Press, 1978.

Kapoor, Gouri Shanker. *Gems and Astrology*. New Delhi: Rajan Publications, 1985.

Kunz, George Frederick. *Rings for the Finger*. New York: Dover Publications, 1973.

Lewis, Roger. *Color and the Edgar Cayce Readings*. Virginia Beach, VA: ARE Press, 1973.

Lorussa, Julia, and Joel Glick. *Healing Stones*. Albuquerque, NM: Mineral Perspectives, Brotherhood of Life, 1979.

Luscher, Max. *The Luscher Color Test*. New York: Random House, 1969.

————. *The Four Color Person*. New York: Pocket Books, 1980.

MacIvor, Virginia, and Sandra Laforest. *Vibrations*. York Beach, ME: Samuel Weiser, Inc, 1979.

Mason, Keith. *Radionics and Progresive Energies*. Essex, UK: C. W. Daniel Co Ltd, 1984.

Pickston, Margaret. *The Language of Flowers*. London: Michael Joseph Ltd, 1968.

Riva, Anna. *Candle Burning Magic*. Toluca Lake, CA: International Imports, 1980.

Tansley, David V. *Radionics and the Subtle Anatomy of Man*. Wellingborough, UK: Health Science Press, 1972.

————. *Twenty-two Gems, Stones and Metals*. Virginia Beach, VA: ARE Press, 1980.

Von Goethe, Johann Wolfgang. *Theory of Colours*. London: John Murray, 1840.

Waite, A. E. *The Complete Manual of Occult Divination*. New Hyde Park, NY: University Books, 1972.

Weeks, Norah. *The Medical Discoveries of Edward Bach*. Essex, UK: C. W. Daniel Co Ltd, 1973.

Yogananda, Paramahansa. *Autobiography of a Yogi*. Los Angeles: Self-Realization Fellowship, 1972.

INDEX

planetary rulership and characteristics of, 75
Friday born, 148–49
Soul Ray compatibilities for,
140, 143, 144–45, 146,
147–48, 149
friends, candle burning ritual for
making of, 82
future events, predicting of,
153

Gemini, 46, 138, 156
gemstones, 163–86, 187
assigned to Apostles, 186
Astrological Health Synthesis
for, 167
astrological signs and, 165–
166
cat's eye, 170–71
coral, 174–75
diamonds, 176–78
emeralds, 179–80, 186
finger for, 168–69
incorrect use of, 163–64, 165
lapis lazuli, 181–82
malachite, 183
mounting of, 168, 186
onyx, 171–72
opals, 184–85
pearls, 172–74
on right vs. left hand, 169
rubies, 169–70
sapphires, 178–79, 186
size of, 168
topaz, 175–76, 186
gender, color and, 30
Genesis (Bible), 15
George, Llewellyn, 161–62
Ghadiali, Darius, 102
Ghadiali, Dinshah P., 58, 101–4,
114, 116
ghosts, candle burning ritual for
exorcising of, 91
Gimbel, Theo, 50, 54, 56
glands:
Astrological Health Synthesis
for, 167

influenced by colors, 103–4
God, worshipped by lighting candles, 72–73
Goethe, Johann Wolfgang von,
40, 43–44, 47, 52
gold, in mythology, 29, 30, 32
Golden Bough, The (Frazer), 43
Golden Gate Bridge (San Francisco), 24
gossip, candle burning ritual for
stopping of, 91–92
Great Book of Magical Art, Hindu
Magic and Indian Occultism,
The (Laurence), 40
Greece, ancient, 31, 37
green, 43–46
astrological signs corresponding to, 138
day of week corresponding to,
123–24
elements associated with, 102–
103
emotions unconsciously associated with, 22–23
envy associated with, 21–22,
43
foods corresponding to, 107–
112
glands stimulated by, 104
legendary figures associated
with, 43
light projection of, 117
musical note and frequency
corresponding to, 120
in mythology, 29, 30, 31, 32,
33
opposite of, 114
personality traits associated
with, 45–46
psychological responses to, 44–
45
psychological states associated
with various shades of, 62–
63
as symbol, 44
vitamins associated with, 104,
105